WHO TOLD YOU THAT?

WHO TOLD YOU THAT?

Overcoming Fear and Failure

BY DR. CHRISTOPHER A. STONE

XULON PRESS

Xulon Press
2301 Lucien Way #415
Maitland, FL 32751
407.339.4217
www.xulonpress.com

Unless otherwise indicated, Scripture quotations taken from the King James Version (KJV) – *public domain.*

Scripture quotations taken from the Amplified Bible (AMP). Copyright © 1954, 1958, 1962, 1964, 1965, 1987 by The Lockman Foundation. Used by permission. All rights reserved.

Printed in the United States of America.

ISBN-13: 978-1-6312-9132-6

TABLE OF CONTENTS

ACKNOWLEDGEMENTS

And he said, Who told you that you were naked?

I first give praise and honor to my Lord and Savior, Jesus Christ. I praise Him for the Spirit of Truth—the Holy Spirit—and for His abiding presence in us who are believers and followers of Jesus Christ. He (the Spirit of Truth) guides us into all truth and shows us all things that God the Father and our Lord and Savior Jesus Christ has for us both now and in the future. "Howbeit when he, the Spirit of truth, is come, he will guide you into all truth; for he shall not speak of himself; but whatsoever he shall hear, that shall he speak; and he will shew you things to come. He shall glorify me; for he shall receive of mine, and shall shew it unto you" (John 16:13–14 KJV).

The Holy Spirit is the teacher and the revealer or "Illuminator" of the hidden truth within Scripture. I thank Him for this truth that He revealed to me over thirty years ago as young believer in Christ who hungered and thirsted to know about the will and ways of God. The Holy Spirit challenged me to question every belief, ideology and thought process that I had to make sure it aligned with His Word. He asked me the question, which is now the title of this book: *Who Told You That?* Although I was Christian, there were many things I believed and thought that were contrary to the Word of God. He told me that as long as my beliefs, ideas, and thoughts were contrary to His Word, the devil—Satan—that serpent of old would always possess the power to control me. The Holy Spirit gave me a desire to know the truth and the truth began to make me free in all areas of my life. I praise God because my desire for His truth has not diminished; in fact, it continues to increase every day.

I also thank my wife, Nadine Stone, for her unwavering honor, love, support, encouragement, and commitment to me for over a quarter of a century. Nadine, you are a rare and special treasure that God has given to remind me of His unconditional love and never-ending mercy. He loved me enough to bestow such honor on me when He gave you to me. I am eternally grateful for you, woman of God; you're my queen.

I thank God for my four beautiful daughters and my sons-in-law, Latisha (Kemontra), their two sons, my grandsons (Karter and Kaleb) Christina (Daniel); Christal (Antonio); Princess (Bryson) and my granddaughter (Kynslee). Wow, God has richly blessed me with His choice treasures when He gave me such wonderful children and grandchildren who are the pride and joy of my life. You all keep my eyes fixed on what is important, focused on what is necessary, and favored by our God. I thank God for each of you. Your love for our God and your desire to serve Him gives me immeasurable joy and peace. Keep pressing for the mark of higher calling in Christ Jesus our Lord!

I would be remiss if I did not thank God for my spiritual father in the gospel ministry, the late Bishop and Dr. Otis Lockett Sr., the founder of the Evangel Fellowship Church of God in Christ, and his wife, First Lady Barbara T. Lockett. I thank God for you and the entire Lockett Family—the late Mother Turner, Faith (James Garner), Otis Jr., and Joshua. What awesome examples of faith, family, fortitude, honor, and integrity you have been for my family and me for over thirty years now. Your character and integrity have and continue to carry nations of people in their faith in Jesus Christ.

I thank God for my leader and mentor, Bishop Patrick L. Wooden Sr. Thank you for your uncompromising stance on the truth of the Word of God and your reverence for the God of the Bible. You are a general in the Lord's army, and your character and integrity are a great source of strength and encouragement in my life. I'll follow you into battle anywhere to fight the good fight of faith in Jesus Christ our Lord. I also thank God First Lady Pamela Wooden, Supervisor Beverly DeJournett, my fellow administrative assistants, and the entire North Carolina Third Ecclesiastical Jurisdiction Family.

I thank God for Dr. Terry Wayne Preslar—founder and president of Gospel Schools of the Bible—and Dr. Dwight Dameron—senior pastor of Faith Baptist Church and lead instructor of Unity Worship Center Bible College. You two men have revolutionized my life through your living examples of faith in Christ, your perseverance through hardships as good soldiers of Christ, your uncompromising stand in teaching the truth of Scripture and your personal friendship and mentorship to me and the church family at Unity Worship Center. I thank God for His divine providence in allowing our paths to cross and establishing such great relationships in us and our ministries. Special thanks to Pastor David Grinnell—Senior Pastor of People's Memorial Church in Burlington, North Carolina, and Dr. Marshall Walker and Robley Kisitu for your editorial review of the original manuscript, your research assistance, and your encouragement in the completion of this project.

Last, but certainly not least I thank God for the Unity Worship Center C.O.G.I.C. church family. You all give me tremendous joy in pastoring. I know that pastoring is not for the faint of heart or weak in spirit, but it is members like you who give me great pleasure in treading out the grain of the Word of God to feed you as sons and daughters of our heavenly Father. Continue to serve the Lord faithfully and seek to do His will in your personal lives, your families, our community, and the world. Thank you for giving me permission and the privilege of leading you on this journey of becoming more like Christ and making disciples throughout the world.

FOREWORD

by
Bishop Patrick L. Wooden Sr.

Y ou are about to be blessed! This is the first thing that comes to my mind to say to all who hold this book in their hands with the intentions of reading it.

Who Told You That? gives in-depth answers to questions regarding fear. Yes, fear. Yet, not the reasonable God-given fear that every human being possesses that protects us. It is reasonable to fear jumping out of a running automobile or to fear putting one's hands to fire. It is reasonable to fear dangerous places and situations. It is proper, right, beneficial and wise to fear God. The Bible says that we are to fear Him that can cast our souls into hell, "And fear not them which kill the body, but are not able to kill the soul: but rather fear him which is able to destroy both soul and body in hell" (Matthew 10:28).

Dr. Stone challenges the wrong kind of fear—the fear that causes one to "quit before we ever get started, it paralyzes our potential and turns God-given visions and dreams into nightmares of reality," as Dr. Stone says.

The Lord Jesus Christ died and rose again to deliver us from, among other things, the wrong kind of fear and to set us free from Satan's paralyzing, debilitating thoughts.

"You can't make it. You're not good enough. You don't measure up. You can't do this. You can't do that." Dr. Stone asks, "who told you that?" Not only does Dr. Stone challenge the devil, but in this book, Dr. Stone gives us God's answers according to God's Truth, which is the written word of God, better known as the Bible.

Dr. Stone is a man of God who has brilliantly written this book from a position of strength—strength because he has and is still living this book and strength because he has walked and *is* walking out this book in his everyday life. His guidepost, his constant source is the Bible. You will read very few sentences in this book without a "Thus saith the Lord." Yes, Dr. Stone is a Bible-man and offers biblical solutions to the questions regarding fear. He has lived and learned that the Scriptures work every time they are applied.

Read this book. Tell others about this book. It will set you free from the wrong kind of fear.

Bishop Patrick L. Wooden, Sr., Prelate

North Carolina Third Ecclesiastical Jurisdiction

INTRODUCTION

And he said, Who told you that you were naked?

Do you ever wonder why we, as human beings, fear and where that fear originated? I'm not talking about the emotion of fear or the feeling that we get when we are surprised or when we see an insect or animal that causes our heart rate to increase, pupils to dilate, and our voices to rise an octave or two. No, I'm talking about the type of fear that is internal; it's not visible to the naked eye and lies deep beneath the surface of our emotions. This fear is mental, and it's a part of our core belief system. It causes us to quit before we even get started, it paralyzes our potential, and it turns God-given visions and dreams into nightmares of reality. This fear holds us in bondage to the opinions and attitudes of others and keeps us hiding behind performance, positions, and even popularity, when all the while we're living in silent frustration.

Do you wonder why is it so easy to fail and so hard to succeed? Again, I'm not talking about failing to complete a task or assignment the first or second time or even when your plans don't turn out exactly as planned. I'm talking about the constant dread of not measuring up and the thought that success always seems to elude you. I'm talking about when you feel like giving up or throwing in the towel at the slightest resistance or opposition. So, you settle in your mind that life is unfair, God is not just, and only certain people get the good breaks in life. I mean a constant failing that causes you to question whether or not God is real, and if He is, does He really care about me? You've become so acquainted with fear and so accustomed to failure that you believe that these experiences are a normal part of life and you just have to live with it.

If you have pondered or asked these or similar questions; you are not abnormal or crazy. You are normal and in your right mind. I believe you have been divinely guided to read this book because God wants to do something miraculous in your life. He wants to change your experiences from doom and gloom to delight and gladness. Hang on a little longer because God, our God, the true and living God, the God who cannot lie; the God who knows you personally and intimately has something He wants to say to you that will revolutionize and totally transform your life. God wants to turn your paralyzing fear and potential-destroying attitude of failure into boldness and success in every area of life. By the time you get finished reading this material, you are going to break through to the real you. You may ask what is a breakthrough? I like the definition that Dr. John Testsola gave as he preached during a Thursday night Bible study at Evangel Fellowship Church of God in Christ in Greensboro, North Carolina. He said a breakthrough is "a sudden burst of knowledge from God that pushes you past all negative resistance or obstacles that once stopped you."

I want to help you to *break* through to become the successful man or woman God created you to be. You are going to discover where this ungodly tormenting fear originated and how it operates. You will also discover its outcome, but most importantly, I want to show you how to overcome it. I want you to experience all the wonderful blessings and promises God has in store for you in this life, and in the life to come, we will enjoy everlasting life in the place Christ has prepared for each of us His children. "The thief comes only in order to steal and kill and destroy. I came that they may have and enjoy life, and have it in abundance [to the full, till it overflows]" (John 10:10 AMP).

Chapter One

BACKGROUND TO THE
PROBLEM OF FEAR

And he said, Who told you that you were naked?

According to the Holy Bible, Adam and his wife partook of the forbidden fruit of the tree of the knowledge of good and evil. Upon doing so, they realized their nakedness, covered themselves with fig leaves, and hid among the trees of the garden of Eden when they heard the Lord's voice (Gen. 3:1–10). What is interesting is that when God called Adam and asked him where he was, Adam responded by saying, "I heard thy voice in the garden, and I was afraid because I was naked; and I hid myself" (vs. 10, KJV). Adam said, "I was afraid." The word "afraid" in this passage of scripture when translated is the Hebrew word *yare* (yaw-ray), which means "to fear; to revere; to frighten; to dread" (Strong, 1984, p. 52). It was fear that caused the first man and woman whom God created to fail to do the will of God for their lives. I contend that it is this same "fear" that also causes many Christians to fail to do the will of God for their lives. The Merriam-Webster Dictionary defines the word "fail" as to prove deficient or lacking; to fall short; to be unsuccessful.

The Inherited Character of Fear

In Genesis 2:15–20, God communicates His will to Adam. It was God's will for Adam to dwell in God's presence in the Garden of Eden (v. 15). It was the will of God for Adam to dress and keep the garden (v. 15). It was the will of God for Adam to eat from the trees of the garden except the tree of the knowledge of good and evil (v. 16). After Adam disobeyed God, he became fearful. This fear caused Adam to fail to do the will of God.

One of the tenets of Christian theology is that all human beings are born with the Adamic nature. Consequently, due to sin human beings are prone to the same failings as the first Adam (Rom. 15:12–14). I will further build upon this point by directing and exploring relevant scriptures in the Holy Bible. In particular, an exegetical analysis of Numbers chapters 13 and 14 will be conducted to explore how the fear that originated with Adam in the Garden of Eden was carried down through the entire nation of Israel. This foreshadows its continuity even in the life of modern-day Christians.

The Continuity of Fear in the Nation of Israel

In Numbers chapters 13 and 14, God instructs the children of Israel to send twelve men (surveyors) from the leadership of their nation into the land of Canaan so they could bring back to the rest of the people a report on the land that God had promised to give unto them and their children. Moses gave the leaders specific instructions as to where they were to go, what they were to inspect, and what they were to bring back from the land as evidence that what God promised them was true. Moses even urged them to be of good courage. However, of the twelve leaders of Israel chosen for this task, ten brought back an evil report of what they had seen in the land of Canaan. Only two of the twelve leaders, Joshua and Caleb, had a good report of what they had seen in the land. Only these two leaders trusted God fully and said to the people of their nation, "Only rebel not ye against the Lord, neither fear ye the people of the land" (Num. 14:9, KJV).

In this Mosaic narrative, the word "fear" translated is the same word that Adam used when he said to God "I was afraid" (Gen. 3:10, KJV). Ten leaders of Israel allowed fear to cause them to bring back an evil report to the rest of the nation of Israel. The nation of Israel allowed the voices of fear that they heard from these leaders to cause them to fail to do what God willed for their lives. According to psychologist Theo Tsaousides (2015), "Fear chokes action and makes you feel vulnerable. You start to question your own abilities, your smarts, your strength, and your potential for success. Your focus shifts from what to do to how to protect yourself. Eventually, you get stalled" (p. 1).

Ten of the twelve spies choked, stalled, and questioned their own potential, regardless of the victories God had promised them. I believe many people are choked and stalled, questioning their own potential because of the voice of fear they've heard or are hearing from leaders in their lives, such as parents, relatives, friends, teachers, coaches, bosses, or supervisors.

Fear Depicted in the Teachings of Jesus

The New Testament, beginning with the teachings of Jesus, supports the belief that this problem of fear is a reason why Christians fail to fulfill God's will in their lives. In the Gospel according to Matthew, the Lord Jesus instructs His followers as to what the kingdom of heaven is to be compared to so they could have a clearer understanding thereof. Jesus tells of a man (a lord, an owner, or a boss) who decides to travel to a far country. Before the man embarks on his journey, he calls three of his servants unto him and gives them money that he wants them to steward while he is away. He gives money to each according to their stewardship abilities. The first servant receives the largest portion of money, the second servant receives the next largest portion, and the third servant receives the smallest amount of money (Matt. 25:14–18).

The Lord leaves and after a long time away he returns. He calls his servants and asks them to give a report of their stewardship over his money. The servant who received the most money reports that he invested the money and now has doubled what the Lord gave him. The owner was very pleased with him. The second servant comes forth and reports likewise; "You gave me this amount of money. I invested it and have received double what you gave me." The Lord was very pleased with him also. The third servant, who received the smallest amount of money, came forth and told his Lord that he did not invest the money he was given because he was afraid, so he still has the same of amount of money that he was given (Matt. 25:14–30, KJV). The word "afraid" used by the servant is the Greek word *phobeo*, (fob-eh'-o), which means "to fear, to be frightful, to be alarmed" (Strong, 1984, p. 76). In Greek, it has the same meaning as the Hebrew word referenced in Genesis 3:10 and Numbers 14:9. The Lord becomes very upset with this servant and calls him wicked and unprofitable. The Lord takes the money from him and gives it to the first servant. The third servant displeases his Lord and is severely punished because his fear caused him to fail to do the will of his master.

I believe that fear is an enemy to the will of God in the lives of Christians. Fear steals God's promises, saps God's power, and stops God's potential; fearful Christians cannot please the Lord, because fear opposes faith. God's word says, "But without faith it is impossible to Him: for he that cometh to God must believe that he is, and that he is a rewarder of them that diligently seek him." (Heb. 11:6, KJV)

My Personal Statement of the Problem of Fear

I became a born-again Christian on Sunday, October 23, 1988 at the age of eighteen. After hearing the Word of God preached by the late Bishop Otis Lockett Sr., I professed faith in the Lord Jesus Christ and accepted Him as Lord and personal Savior at Evangel Fellowship Word

Ministries located at 507 Balboa Street, Greensboro, North Carolina at approximately 1:30 p.m.

At the time of this writing (2019), I am forty-nine years old and have been a disciple of Christ for more than thirty years. I have been married for twenty-six years and have four daughters, four sons-in-law, and three grandchildren. I was ordained as a minister at the age of twenty-one; graduated from college with a degree in public administration at the age of twenty-two; married at the age of twenty-three; served as the youth pastor at a church of over 3,000 members at age twenty-four; ordained as an elder in the Church of God in Christ at age twenty-eight; commissioned to plant and serve as senior pastor of a church at age thirty. I have helped plant three other churches out of the church I pioneered and have been pastoring a local church I founded for over eighteen years. I have been blessed to travel to different parts of the United States and foreign countries to preach and teach the Word of God and meet many people, Christians and non-Christians alike. I presently talk with and disciple Christians from various backgrounds and experiences in life. One consistent theme I continue to discover when I meet, disciple, and lead people is that many of them have failed or are failing to do the will of God in areas of their lives because of fear.

Before becoming a Christian, I was reared in a very sinful environment by non-Christian parents. I received some positive but mostly negative psychological and physiological characteristics from my parents. Noted biologist and zoologist Edwin Grant Conklin refers to this as "nature," the genetically controlled qualities of an organism (Conklin, 2011, p. 57). I was impacted and influenced by my environmental and social surroundings. In social science, this is known as "nurture," which is the sum of the environmental factors influencing the behavior and traits expressed by an organism (Merriam-Webster Dictionary).

I had good and bad, and right and wrong subconscious beliefs, ideologies, and values that I had been taught and others I caught. I developed certain perceptions, feelings, and adaptive behaviors as a result of the cultural, ethnic, and social stimuli I received. As a result, I developed psychological and emotional coping mechanisms to adapt to my environment. I learned and practiced some of the same devastating and destructive beliefs and behaviors as the people with whom I was reared and associated. I developed irrational fears and habits that I learned later in life were unfounded and unhealthy.

I doubted myself and lived with a consistent feeling that I was letting people down who were important to me and failing to deliver on promises. Dr. Theo Tsaousides calls these feelings the fear of failure. "If you *think* you are in danger, the fear response sequence becomes activated. When you think something is dangerous, scary, impossible to handle, an obstacle, a problem that exceeds your abilities, your brain will continue to treat it that way. And that's what self-doubt is" (Tsaousides, 2015, p. 11). I became a habitual self-doubter and someone who lacked personal confidence.

I became a born-again Christian on October 23, 1988. I began reading, studying, and receiving teaching from the Holy Bible. As a result, I began to change my thinking, beliefs, and actions. I began to be "transformed by the renewing of my mind" by the Word of God (Rom. 12:2, KJV). I began to see how the attitudes, beliefs, and ideologies I learned, developed, and practiced for years before becoming a Christian had produced certain subconscious perceptions and actions that caused me difficulty and sometimes produced repetitive rebellions against the Word of God in areas of my developing faith. I was deeply convicted by these attitudes and actions and sought the Lord in prayer and fasting for a change.

For the first few years of my new life in Christ, I believed these actions were unique to me, and I often felt misunderstood and alone. I later learned through the study of the Word of God that this was not true. On the contrary, I discovered that many people who were called by God, loved by God, and anointed by God suffered from the devastating effects of fear when they tried to fulfill the will of God for their lives. I began to search Scripture diligently to find help for my plight. Through my past and present interactions and communication with Christians from various ages, backgrounds, cultures, denominational affiliations, and experiences, I have learned that many of them also suffer from similar psychological fears that hinder them from doing the will of God in their lives. I've discovered how they too have learned to live in silent frustration, condemnation, guilt, and shame.

Statement of Purpose

The purpose of this book is to assess the prevalence and causes of five major psychological fears identified among people, specifically Christians, of various ages, cultures, denominational affiliations, ethnicities, and life experiences that cause failure in fulfilling the will of God in areas of life and help them overcome these fears.

William Gurnall states:

A cowardly spirit is beneath the lowest duty of Christians. You of all men will need courage and determination if you hope to obey your Heavenly Captain's orders. He commands you, Be thou strong and very courageous. . . . Why? So you can stand in battle against warlike nations? So you can make a great name for yourself? No! But , . . . "that thou mayest observe to do according to all the law, which Moses, my servant commanded thee" (Gurnall, 2014, p. 24).

One of the most important tasks assigned to the brain is to protect human beings from danger and keep them safe. When the brain registers threat, it activates the sympathetic nervous system, the part of the nervous system that controls the body's acute stress response, which is probably known by its more popular name: fight-or-flight response. The term "fight or flight response" was first used in 1929 by Walter Cannon to describe how animals respond to threat. Over the years, researchers studying the fight or flight reaction extended it to humans and expanded it to include a sequence of four possible reactions: freeze, fight, flight, or fright, or the 4F response (Braha, 2004). The acute stress response known as fright, which means you do nothing, is the response that causes Christians to fail to fulfill the will of God for their lives. I discovered that most people have five prominent, psychological fears. These fears are death, loneliness, loss, pain, and rejection. Each fear will be discussed more in depth throughout the book.

Why do human beings experience fear, and what is the origin of their fear? This book is not about the emotion of fear or the feeling that human beings get when they are surprised unexpectedly, or when they see an insect or an animal that causes the human heart rate to increase, pupils to dilate and voices to rise an octave or two. This type of fear is known as dread, "which is based on a genuine danger" this is normal and natural (Pfister, Christianity and fear: A study in history and in the psychology and hygiene of religion, 1948, p. 43).

Instead, the focus of this book is on fear that is abnormal and internal—the type of fear that is not visible to the naked eye but lies deep beneath the surface of our emotions. This fear is psychological and is part of the core belief systems of people. It causes a person to quit before ever getting started, it paralyzes potential and turns God-given visions and dreams into nightmares of reality. Pfister gives some examples of such fear. "Instances occur when a man continually dreads a fearful catastrophe without being able to adduce any real reason, when a girl jumps screaming on the table with every sign of intense fear on seeing a mouse; or when a man is unceasingly terrified from early youth to extreme old age by the figure 13 and is compelled to carry on a painful struggle until he is released from his torments by looking at a church tower" (Pfister, 1913, p. 70). This fear holds human beings in bondage to the opinions and attitudes of others and keeps them comatose in conduct while living in camouflaged frustration. "Fear immobilizes its victim—like the distraught soldier who runs trembling to his foxhole at first rumor of an attack and refuses to come out until all threat of danger is past" (Gurnall, 2014, p. 23).

As I stated in the introduction, one may wonder why at certain times fear seizes certain people and failure is a consistent companion and close comrade? Why is it so easy to fail and so hard to succeed? The fear explored in this book reveals itself in the consistent belief of some people that they cannot measure up and thus think that success will always be just out of reach. That unconscious state of mind causes human beings to see themselves as victims of bad breaks and unfortunate circumstances. The findings of this research and revelation will contribute to the Christians' ability to discover how to identify and overcome fear to achieve breakthrough and successfully fulfill the will of Almighty God for their lives in areas of past failure.

Chapter Two

THE ORIGIN OF FEAR

And he said, Who told you that you were naked?

I n chapter 3 of Genesis, God allows the reader of the Bible to witness the origin and effects of sin as it is introduced to mankind (Adam and his wife) in the Garden of Eden, where God had placed them. This introduction of sin is believed to be the source of irrational fear. It is why mankind struggles with what's known as irrational fear and failure. I believe that sin is the source of fear and one of the primary causes of Christians' failure to fulfill the will of God in various areas of their lives.

This chapter takes a closer look at this problem of sin and fear that plagues so many, especially those who have been "saved by grace through faith" through the blood of Jesus Christ and are called Christians. (Eph. 2:8, KJV). We begin with the description of the fall from Genesis:

> Now the serpent was more subtil than any beast of the field which the LORD God had made. And he said unto the woman, Yea, hath God said, Ye shall not eat of every tree of the garden? And the woman said unto the serpent, We may eat of the fruit of the trees of the garden: But of the fruit of the tree which is in the midst of the garden, God hath said, Ye shall not eat of it, neither shall ye touch it, lest ye die. And the serpent

said unto the woman, Ye shall not surely die: For God doth know that in the day ye eat thereof, then your eyes shall be opened, and ye shall be as gods, knowing good and evil. And when the woman saw that the tree was good for food, and that it was pleasant to the eyes, and a tree to be desired to make one wise, she took of the fruit thereof, and did eat, and gave also unto her husband with her; and he did eat. And the eyes of them both were opened, and they knew that they were naked; and they sewed fig leaves together, and made themselves aprons. And they heard the voice of the LORD God walking in the garden in the cool of the day: and Adam and his wife hid themselves from the presence of the LORD God amongst the trees of the garden (Genesis 3:1–11, KJV).

In this passage of Scripture, the serpent was, in the beginning, the most intelligent and cunning creature the Lord had created of all the land animals or reptiles. The serpent in and of itself is not bad or evil, but Satan, the enemy of God, used this creature to introduce his diabolical plan of rebellion and disobedience to mankind. Since Satan is a created being and not a creator like God, he had to use the God-given ability of the serpent to entice or tempt the woman, the weaker vessel of the two human beings in the garden (1 Pet. 3:7, KJV). The phrase "weaker vessel" means that she is not as physically strong as the man. God made the man physically stronger because he was given the assignment to work or till the ground and provide for the family. It does not mean that she (the woman) is less important than the man; she is simply distinctly different based upon her assignment from God. Anatomically and physiologically, women have great strength because they are able carry and give birth to children. This is one of the distinct things that women can do that men cannot. However, men genetically have approximately thirty-five percent more muscle mass than women, which simply means that generally males are physically stronger than females. And what also settles the issue that she (the woman) is the weaker vessel is because the Word of God says she is.

I would now like to highlight biblical creation as it relates to the subject of men and women or male and female because now there is much debate, division, and confusion among people about how to identify people as man or woman. The reason for such debate and division on this subject will be discussed in more detail in the next chapter. However, at this time, I would like to point out that according to Scripture and science, a human being who does not have a womb is not a female, he is a male. It doesn't matter what he believes, what physiological changes he has made to himself, how he dresses, talks, and behaves, or what the modernistic, politically correct culture says; he is male. Male is defined as an individual of the sex that is typically capable of producing small, usually motile gametes (such as sperm or spermatozoa) that fertilize the eggs of a female (Merriam-Webster Dictionary). If a human being has a womb, she is a female, not a male. Again, no matter what she believes, what physiological changes she makes to herself, how she dresses, talks, and behaves or what the modernistic, politically correct culture says, she is female. Female is defined as being the sex that typically has the capacity to bear young or produce eggs (Merriam-Webster Dictionary).

God created woman with a womb and the ability to give birth based upon her created assignment. Likewise, God created man stronger physically based upon his created assignment.

Satan used the serpent to speak to and tempt the woman. Again, Satan is a created being and cannot create, but because he is a crafty strategist, he uses the same strategies or tactics against the followers of Christ. He will seek to tempt human beings when they are in their weakest state emotionally, mentally, or physically. According to Scripture, Satan is the tempter and the evil one, not the serpent as a created reptile:

And when the tempter came to him, he said, If thou be
the Son of God, command that these stones be made
bread (Matthew 4:3, KJV).

Jesus answered them, "Did I not choose you, the
Twelve? And [yet] one of you is a devil [of the evil one
and a false accuser]" (John 6:70, AMP).

And the great dragon was cast out, that old serpent,
called the Devil, and Satan, which deceiveth the whole
world: he was cast out into the earth, and his angels
were cast out with him (Revelation 12:9, KJV).

And he laid hold on the dragon, that old serpent, which
is the Devil, and Satan, and bound him a thousand *years*
(Revelation 20:2, KJV).

The point here is that people should not have a hatred for snakes
or serpents in and of themselves as reptiles. They are simply creatures
created by God and they serve a very important role in our ecological
system. Mankind, however, should hate Satan and his ways. The devil
sought to get his plan of sin and rebellion in this earthly realm, and the
only way that it could happen was through the man and woman God
had created in His image who had been given dominion on earth (Gen.
1:26–28). They were also the ones to whom God had given His words
and instructions. Therefore, Satan uses the serpent to carry out his plan
to tempt the ones with God's assignment and God's authority on the
earth into disobeying God's command.

Satan tempts all mankind to rebel against the will of God by encouraging people to put human desire above God's desire. A. B. Simpson
said, "Then comes self-indulgence, doing a thing because you like to do
it. No man has a right to do a thing for the pleasure it affords, because
he enjoys or likes it. I have no right to take my dinner just because I

like it. This makes me a beast. I do it because it nourishes me. Doing things because they please yourself, seeking your own interest, is wrong. 'Seek ye first the kingdom of God, and his righteousness.' We have no Divine warrant to seek ourselves in anything. Seek God, and God will seek your good. Take care of the things of God, because He will take care of you. Look not any man on your own things, but on the things of others" (2011, p. 5).

Satan uses God's image on the earth (mankind) to give birth to sin through temptation. He (Satan) says to the woman "Yea, hath God said, Ye shall not eat of every tree of the garden?" (Gen. 3:1, KJV). I previously stated that Satan is a created being and thus cannot create anything new. What he did to tempt the first man and woman to sin, he also did when trying to tempt Jesus Christ during His forty days of fasting in the wilderness, and he does the same to tempt the followers of Christ presently. He used the natural desires of the woman to tempt her, and he tried to do so with Jesus Christ during his earthly ministry following His water baptism and ministerial affirmation from the Father and Holy Spirit in Matthew 3:16–17 and Matthew 4:1–10.

In Genesis 3:1 (KJV), Satan said to the woman "Yea, hath God said, Ye shall not eat of every tree of the garden?" Later, the tempter (Satan) said unto Christ Jesus, "If thou be the Son of God, command that these stones be made bread" (Matt. 4:3, KJV). Henceforth, this exploration will use the terminology "first Adam and last Adam," for Scripture says in "Thus it is written, The first man Adam became a living being (an individual personality); the last Adam (Christ) became a life-giving Spirit [restoring the dead to life" (1 Cor. 15:45).

In each case, with both the first Adam and last Adam; Satan did the following:

1) He tried to get them to **doubt or question** the Word of God. In twenty-first century English, he (Satan) said to them as he does to Christians, can you really trust that the Word of God (The

Holy Bible) is authoritative, infallible and inerrant? How do you really know you can trust the Word of God? Satan introduced doubt to the authority of the Word of God to the woman. He said to Jesus, if you really are who you say you are (God in the flesh) prove it? Satan attempted to tempt Christ Jesus, the Word of God made flesh (incarnate) to *doubt or question* who He was. If Jesus would have given into the temptation to prove He was God by making the stones bread to satisfy His physical hunger, Satan would have been successful in his temptation in causing Jesus to doubt or question that He was God. Jesus Christ was 100% God while in His humanity. He suffered hunger, fatigue, frustration and weakness while on earth, but He was still 100% God. He needed not to prove that He was God to doubters because He was, is and will always be God whether anyone believes or not. Satan was fully aware of this, but it did not stop him in his futile temptation of Christ because he is the tempter. He can only do what he is, tempt, deceive, steal, kill, and destroy. He does the same to followers of Christ. He tempts by creating doubt to the reality of God and the authority of His Word. Scripture shows that Satan can speak in both the first person singular; he can also speak in the second person plural and in many other forms of verbal and non-verbal communication. He has a voice and he does speak deceptively to those whom he is seeking to deceive. He is a liar and the father of lies. He lies to people about themselves and he lies to people about other people. He is a liar, any and everything he says is a lie (John 8:44). He lies to people about God and he lies to people about what God has said to them and about them in the Word of God, the Holy Bible. The child of God must trust in the absolute authority of the written text of the Holy Bible. "The Bible is to be believed not debated on the field of intellectual combat. The blessing is in it being trusted" (Preslar, 2002, p. 6).

2) He tried to get them to ***disregard*** or ***qualify*** the Word of God. In the garden of Eden, "the serpent said unto the woman, 'Ye shall not surely die'" (Gen. 3:4, KJV), Satan also said to Jesus Christ, "If thou be the Son of God, cast thyself down; for it is written, He shall give his angels charge concerning thee; and in their hands they shall bear thee up, lest at any time thou dash thy foot against a stone" (Matt. 4:6, KJV). In both cases again with the first Adam and the last Adam, Satan's temptation was to disregard or qualify the Word of God. He tells the woman, "Ye shall not surely die" and he said unto Jesus, "cast thyself down; for it is written, He shall give his angels charge concerning thee." Satan said to them what he says to people today; disregard what God says, and disregard the authority of the Word of God because God does not mean what He says. God will make an exception to His Word; the rules given then do not apply now. The devil also says there are special revelations, special relationships, and special rules that are different from person to person and in various situations. Everyone has their own truth. I say emphatically . . .*no, no, no*! God means what He says; He is not unclear as to what He means when He speaks. There is no such thing as special revelation, special relationships, or special rules with God for some and not for others. There is only one truth, God's truth, and it is found in the Word of God and in the person of Jesus Christ. In John 14:6 (KJV) it says, "Jesus saith unto him, I am the way, the truth, and the life; no man cometh unto the Father, but by me." The devil wants people to think they can disregard or qualify what God says based upon situations, circumstances, or life experiences. He (God) means what He says anytime and all the time. To doubt and disagree with God's Word is a trick of Satan that will lead to death and destruction.

In Genesis 3:5 (KJV) Satan said to the woman, "For God doth know that in the day ye eat thereof, then your eyes shall be opened, and ye shall be as gods, knowing good and evil." In Matthew 4:8–9 (KJV) it states, "Again, the devil taketh him up into an exceeding high mountain, and sheweth him all the kingdoms of the world, and the glory of them; And saith unto him, All these things will I give thee, if thou wilt fall down and worship me." Finally, in both cases with the first Adam and last Adam, Satan attempts to get them to:

3) **Disagree** or **quarrel** with God and His Word. Satan said to the woman, "God knows that when you eat your eyes will be opened, and you will be as gods" (Gen. 3:5, KJV). Satan says to Jesus Christ, "All these things will I give thee, if you will fall down and worship me" (Matthew 4:9, KJV). In the temptations of both the woman in the Garden and Jesus Christ in the wilderness, Satan said to them what he also says to people today: Don't do things God's way. There is another way, a better way than God's way. It is okay to disagree with God and the Word of God, because as mankind you are gods and don't need God. The devil says to mankind, "Make your own decisions, run your lives independently of God, and don't let God interfere with your life." Modernists believe the Holy Bible is outdated and antiquated and that only brainwashed fanatics follow such nonsense. Who gives these preachers or pastors the right to tell people how to live? Look at man's technology, innovation, and information—why trust something that can't be seen when we can trust ourselves.

William Gurnall says, "The philosophy called humanism has long been a suitor to man's pride. It boasts in his natural strength and wisdom, and woos him with promises of grand accomplishments now, and heaven later" (Gurnall, 2014, p. 41).

These are the schemes of the devil; he cannot change his ways. He tempted the first Adam and the last Adam in the same ways, and he also tempts those who are made in the image of God and who are the ambassadors of Christ. Satan's ultimate plan is to get mankind to disobey or rebel against God and His Word. This is how he was successful in introducing sin into the world through the first Adam, but thanks be to God that Jesus Christ, the last Adam, was in all points tempted as are all human beings, but, yet He did not yield to the temptation by sinning against God the Father (Heb. 4:15).

Christians have a high priest in Jesus Christ who has paid the full price for their redemption from sin. He has given an example that shows what Christians' attitudes should be toward sin and how His followers ought to live. Jesus Christ has sent the Holy Spirit and given His abiding presence and power so that the child of God can live victoriously over sin (John 14:15–17).

I believe irrational fear originated with the sin of disobedience by the first created human beings—Adam and his wife. According to von Balthasar, "Anxiety is immanent in the mind, but he sees the ultimate root of this immanence, not in man's finitude, but in a disorder caused by original sin" (von Balthasar, 1989, p. 24). Satan tempted mankind, they yielded to the temptation, and now the "lusts of the flesh, the lusts of the eyes and the pride of life" are things that all mankind must contend while on earth. These things are in the world and at the heart of all mankind (1 John 2:16, KJV).

Scripture declares "And when the woman saw that the tree was good for food [lust of the flesh], and that it was pleasant to the eyes [lust of the eyes], and a tree to be desired to make one wise [pride of life], she took of the fruit thereof, and did eat, and gave also unto her husband with her; and he did eat" (Gen. 3:6, KJV). Satan successfully deceived and planted the seed of disobedience and rebellion in the heart of mankind, and yes, I said mankind, male and female. I emphasize this point because I have heard some men say as Adam said in the beginning; "The woman you gave me," so it's the woman's fault that we're in this mess

(Gen. 3:12, KJV). The Word of God tells us that he [Adam] was with his wife during the time she was being spoken to by the serpent. Pay close attention to what the Scriptures say. "She took of the fruit thereof, and did eat, and gave also unto her husband *with her*; and he did eat" (Gen. 3:6, KJV, emphasis added).

Adam was there with his wife and he knew what God had said to him by way of His commandment according to Genesis 2:16–17. The woman was deceived by Satan, but the man [Adam] chose to disobey. They both doubted, disregarded, and disagreed with God and His Word and finally they disobeyed the command of God. This action created a division between mankind and their Creator (God), which introduced death and destruction to every good thing that God placed under the dominion of mankind. Andrew Collier says, "With the fall, things that had previously been united fall apart into a war of all against all, species against species, person against person, bodily organ against bodily organ. Each entity becomes at once *destructive* because it is set against other entities in a struggle for existence, and *destructible* since its parts no longer cohere but tend to fall apart and hence become vulnerable to the aggression of other individuals." (Collier, 2003, p. 106)

Adam and his wife hid from the presence of God among the trees of the garden because of fear. They failed in a hopeless attempt to cover the nakedness of their flesh with fig leaves (Gen. 3:7–8, KJV).

The Word of God reveals that the original sin of disobedience was the origin of fear and the cause of mankind's failure to fulfill the will of God in the beginning. This same fear continues to cause many to fail to fulfill the will of God for lives now. In the next chapter, I will discuss the operation of fear and specific causes of fear.

Chapter Three

THE OPERATION OF FEAR

And he said, Who told you that you were naked?

In chapter two, the origin of fear was discussed and shown to be the result of the sin of the first man and woman (Gen. 3). In this chapter, I describe the operation of fear and its effect in the lives of people. I want to expose how irrational fear can devastate the lives of people, especially Christians.

Fear divides and distorts vision. It perverts or twists normal behavior and thinking into that which is abnormal and dysfunctional. I believe that irrational fear is one of the many schemes of Satan's diabolical plan for all mankind. He desires that mankind remain under the control of fear and live in an ongoing cycle of failure. Satan does not want people to understand nor operate in their God-given purpose nor tap into God's true power and potential for their lives. Satan hates when people discover their purpose, potential, and power in God.

Satan was successful in causing the first Adam and his wife to give in to his schemes. They took the bait, and as a result, all mankind thereafter has been in bondage to sin. All people since the fall of the first man and woman are born with the "Adamic nature," which is the nature to sin or rebel against God and His Word. "For all have sinned, and come short of the glory of God" (Rom. 3:23, KJV).

Scripture declares "For as in Adam all die, even so in Christ shall all be made alive" (1 Cor. 15:22, KJV). This means that the Adamic or sinful nature of mankind will produce death, both physically and spiritually. But thanks be to God for the last Adam—Jesus Christ—who conquered both sin and death, through His sinless life, sacrificial death and supernatural resurrection. He defeated sin in the flesh. "He personally bore our sins in His [own] body on the tree [as on an altar and offered Himself on it], that we might die [cease to exist] to sin and live to righteousness. By His wounds you have been healed" (1 Pet. 2:24, AMP).

Scripture says "And the eyes of them both were opened, and they knew that they were naked; and they sewed fig leaves together, and made themselves aprons. And they heard the voice of the Lord God walking in the garden in the cool of the day: and Adam and his wife hid themselves from the presence of the Lord God amongst the trees of the garden. And the Lord God called unto Adam, and said unto him, Where art thou? And he said, I heard thy voice in the garden, and I was afraid, because I was naked; and I hid myself" (Gen. 3:7–10, KJV).

The operation of fear as a result of sin in the lives of mankind can be understood in these passages of Scripture. Irrational fear has a very definite and devastating effect on the lives of people who are under its control. These effects are threefold:

1.) Dysfunctional
2.) Divisive
3.) Destructive

Adam and his wife partook of the fruit from the tree of the knowledge of good and evil, and "The eyes of them both were opened, and they knew they were naked; and they sewed fig leaves together, and made themselves aprons" (Gen. 3:7, KJV).

After disobeying God and becoming sinful, they became fear-filled and began immediately to fail to fulfill God's will and original intent for their lives. They became *dysfunctional.* They began to deviate from their original purpose and ceased to function according to their original design. When something or someone is dysfunctional, it is "marked by impaired abnormal functioning; characterized by abnormal or unhealthy interpersonal behavior or interaction (Merriam-Webster Dictionary). I believe the operation of fear in the lives of people causes dysfunction. Adam and his wife "Sewed fig leaves together and made themselves aprons" (Gen. 3:7, KJV).

The actions of the first man and woman became dysfunctional as a result of fear. God provided the fig tree and many other trees in the Garden of Eden as a source of food for them to eat. The trees and their substance were for mankind's ingestion and digestion for nourishment and physical well-being. The effects of fear in their lives caused them to pull the leaves from the trees and cover themselves. They took the leaves from their life source, the tree. They attempted to cover their disobedience, doubt, and disgust with themselves. They used the leaves for a purpose for which they had not been created because they were no longer fulfilling the purpose for which they had been created. This dysfunctional behavior is caused by a life under the control of fear as a result of sin. I believe people who are under the control of sin have no choice but to fear and fail to fulfill their God-given purpose through dysfunctional cycles.

When people are in dysfunctional cycles as a result of fear, they also cause many other things that God has created to become dysfunctional. Sinful man has successfully created dysfunctional marriages, children, families, finances, churches, careers, communities, and governments—a very dysfunctional world. These dysfunctions are a direct result of sin, which leads to fear and failure. I believe this dysfunction as a result fear is the reason many men fail to be the godly leaders they were created to be; why some women feel as though they have to compete with men instead of fulfilling their purpose to help complete the man they have become one with in holy matrimony. I believe it's why some people are confused about their sexual identity and orientation, and why many seek power and positions, instead of purpose and piety.

I challenge the reader to take a moment to pause and think about your past life of sin and how dysfunctional you, your family members, friends, and associates were. Reflect for a moment on the actions you and they engaged in, along with attitudes and behaviors that were contrary to God's purpose and plan. The child of God must not forget the destructive nature of sin and how we covered up, pretended, and deceived people, trying to appear to be someone we were not. Think about the hatred, lies, pain, offenses, and abuse inflicted upon ourselves and others. Satan's plan for all mankind is for them to remain dysfunctional all the days of their lives due to fear. He wants these and other patterns of behavior to continue to operate even after people become born-again children of God. He (Satan) wants Christians to continue to be dysfunctional due to fear although they are "new creatures in Christ" (2 Cor. 5:17, KJV).

I believe it is vital for people to understand the operation of fear as a result of sin and receive the grace of God through the redeeming blood of Jesus Christ to cleanse them from all sin (past, present, and future). Christians must be determined to live in the freedom in which Christ Jesus purchased through His death on the cross. "If the Son therefore shall make you free, ye shall be free indeed" (John 8:36, KJV).

The second operation of fear is seen in Genesis 3:8 (KJV), which states, "They heard the voice of the Lord God walking in the garden in the cool of the day; and Adam and his wife hid themselves from the presence of the Lord God amongst the trees of the garden."

After disobeying the Lord's command, Adam and his wife became not only dysfunctional but also ***divided.*** They became separated from the presence of God. The sinful state caused by fear divided their faith and focus away from God. In this context, the word divided means "disagreeing with each other; disunited; directly or moved toward conflicting interests, states, or objects (Merriam-Webster Dictionary). I believe the operation of fear through sin seeks to divide and separate people, especially Christians, from God. Sin causes a detachment from the source of our purpose and power—God. "Adam and his wife hid themselves from the presence of the Lord God amongst the trees of the garden" (Gen. 3:8, KJV).

When they heard the voice of God, instead of running to God, they ran away from God. Instead of walking in the light, they operated in the divisive work of darkness. Again, this is how people who are controlled by fear operate. They are divided or separated from God. The "measure of faith" that has been given to trust God and His Word becomes divided between human ability, worldly wisdom, and the strength of the flesh (Rom. 12:3).

This is what Satan desires; he does not want people to depend totally on God, trust God totally, or cast all their cares on Him. Satan wants people to move further and further away from God into the darkness of sin and deception so they can stay divided—not only divided and detached from God but divided from and against one another. Nations of people and cultures have been and are currently divided. Countries, communities, and families are divided. Friendships are divided because of the divisive work of sin in the hearts of mankind. This operation of fear causes failure to do the will of God, which erodes the very foundation of trust in God, which leaves many helpless as they continue trying to cover up and hide from the true source of life in Christ.

> "Come unto me, all ye that labour and are heavy laden, and I will give you rest. Take my yoke upon you, and learn of me; for I am meek and lowly in heart; and ye shall find rest unto your souls. For my yoke is easy, and my burden is light" (Matthew 11:28–30, KJV).

God wants mankind to come to Him; Satan wants mankind to stay away from God. He wants to keep Christians divided from their Lord and Savior—Jesus Christ—through guilt, condemnation, and shame. Children of God and followers of Jesus Christ do not have to yield to temptation nor sin against God, but if they do, they must learn to run to God not away from Him. Christians should not hide in guilt, shame, or condemnation. That is a satanic trick. The child of God must learn to run to the One who loves them with an everlasting love and who stands ready to forgive and receive them into His loving outstretched arms.

> "The Lord hath appeared of old unto me, saying, Yea, I have loved thee with an everlasting love; therefore with lovingkindness have I drawn thee" (Jeremiah 31:3, KJV).

> "If we confess our sins, he is faithful and just to forgive us our sins, and to cleanse us from all unrighteousness" (1 John 1:9, KJV).

The third and final operation of fear as a result of sin is described in the book of Genesis, which states, "And the Lord God called unto Adam, and said unto him, Where art thou?" (Gen. 3:9). Adam and his wife sinned by disobeying the command of the Lord and in doing so mankind became dysfunctional, then divided, and finally ***destructive.***

Adam and his wife were not where they normally communed with God, nor were they doing what they were created to do. They were created to be fruitful, multiply, replenish, subdue, dominate, and govern. "And God blessed them, and God said unto them, 'Be fruitful, and multiply, and replenish the earth, and subdue it; and have dominion over the fish of the sea, and over the fowl of the air, and over every living thing that moveth upon the earth'" (Gen. 1:28, KJV).

Instead of giving life and ruling as the image of God in the earthly realm, they became destructive in their purpose. They were not in the presence of God; as a matter of fact, they were hiding from God's presence, and God asked them where they were. Why? Because they were not where they should have been and they were not doing what they had been created to do. They were taking life by pulling figs leaves from their life source to cover their nakedness; this was and is destructive behavior. The word destructive means ruinous; designed or tending to hurt or destroy (Merriam-Webster Dictionary).

They hid from the presence of God—destructive behavior. They were not using their God-given abilities to tend, cultivate, multiply, and replenish—again, destructive behavior. Instead of giving life, they were causing death. They attempted to cover the nakedness of the flesh with dying fig leaves. I believe this is a picture of what was going on inside them; their relationship with God was dying because their fellowship with Him was broken through disobedience. Just as those fig leaves were dying on their flesh because they had been separated from the branches of the tree, the spirits of Adam and his wife were dying because they'd been separated from their source—God. They were now being controlled by fear.

> The Lord said to His disciples, "Abide in me, and I in you. As the branch cannot bear fruit of itself, except it abide in the vine; no more can ye, except ye abide in me" (John 15:4, KJV).

Adam and his wife were created to live in the presence of God. The Garden of Eden was also known as the Garden of God, the place of God's habitation on earth. The tree of life and the tree of the knowledge of good and evil were in the midst of this garden. God walked in this garden, and there He communed with Adam and his wife. Everything they needed was in the Garden of God. Christians should understand that all they need is in God's presence. There is no satisfaction, no peace, nor contentment for the child of God unless it is in God's presence. Christians will not find peace or lasting pleasure in the world nor in anything the world offers. Adam and his wife lost vital union with God when they sinned. They ran away from God's presence and the source of life. They aborted their purpose, abused their potential, and averted God's plan; they became dysfunctional, divided, and destructive.

Satan wants Christians to stop abiding in Christ, so they'll become fruitless and destructive. The Lord wants His followers to bear fruit—to look, live, and love like Christ. If Christians fail to abide in the presence of God because of fear, as Adam and his wife did, they too will cease to fulfill their purpose and become destructive. After sinning, Adam and his wife were not fruitful, nor were they multiplying and replenishing the earth with the image of God. To the contrary, they perpetuated darkness, deception, and death. I have witnessed such actions in the lives of some people who confess to be Christians. I believe Satan has many confessing Christians, but not practicing Christians deceived because they don't understand the operation of fear and the failure it produces.

Christians must gain a better understanding of how Satan wants to continue his diabolical and destructive plan in their lives. The child of God must resist him (Satan) steadfastly in the faith and abide in the presence of God so they can be the fruitful representatives of the Lord in the earth. The anointed men and women of God must do as Jesus did when He walked the earth. The child of God must seek to "go about doing good, healing all who are oppressed by the devil" (Acts 10:38, KJV).

God is with His followers and Christians have an unction (anointing) from the Holy One, Jesus Christ, (1 John 2:20) and the power of the Holy Ghost (Acts 1:8 KJV).

I believe Christians can win over sin and fulfill God's plan and purpose for their lives. God is with His followers, and children of God have His anointing and power at work within them and can defeat the effects of the operation of fear. In chapter four, I describe how the outcome of fear results in failure to fulfill the will of God.

Chapter Four

THE OUTCOME OF FEAR

And he said, Who told you that you were naked?

The Word of God says that after Adam and his wife ate of the fruit of the tree of the knowledge of good and evil and "the eyes of them both were opened, and they knew that they were naked; and they sewed fig leaves together, and made themselves aprons" (Gen. 3:7, KJV).

In chapters two and three, I discussed the origin and the operation of fear as a result of sin. In this chapter, I am going to describe the outcome of fear. If mankind lives in disobedience to the revealed will of God, it is sin, and the outcome will be a life controlled by fear which produces failure to fulfill the will of God. Scripture tells us that the "wages [payment, result, or outcome] of sin is death" (Rom. 6:23, KJV).

As a result of Adam and his wife's disobedience to God in partaking of the fruit of tree of the knowledge of good and evil, mankind became sinful creatures. The desire of sin is to rule mankind, but God wants mankind to rule over sin.

> "And the Lord said unto Cain, Why art thou wroth? And why is thy countenance fallen? If thou doest well, shalt thou not be accepted? And if thou doest not well, sin lieth at the door. And unto thee shall be his desire, and thou shalt rule over him" (Gen. 4:6–7, KJV).

The reality is, however, that unredeemed, unregenerate mankind cannot rule over sin. They are the slaves of sin, totally controlled by sin's desires and doomed to receive sin's deadly outcome—fear and failure. The only hope for mankind is redemption through the atoning blood of Jesus Christ. "But God be thanked, that ye were the servants of sin, but ye have obeyed from the heart that form of doctrine which was delivered you. Being then made free from sin, ye became the servants of righteousness" (Rom. 6:17–18, KJV).

There are some people who have a confession of faith in Jesus Christ as Savior, but do not a have profession of faith in Him as Lord [Master and Ruler]. A profession involves a paid occupation, especially one that involves prolonged training and a formal qualification (Merriam-Webster Dictionary).

Christians are not paid in monetary funds for following Christ as one who works in a specific occupation; however, they are given grace to carry out the responsibilities given to them by the Lord, which is immensely greater than any amount of monetary payment. Profession of faith involves a commitment to practice obedience to God and His Word through disciplined training in the Word of God, and consistent acts of righteousness which originate from a truly redeemed heart that recognizes Jesus Christ as both Lord and Savior. This is what Scripture means when it says, "But you obeyed from the heart that form of doctrine which was delivered you. Being then made free from sin, ye became the servants of righteousness" (Rom. 6:17–18, KJV). If there is not a commitment from the Christian to obey the Word of God from the heart, there will be the presence of fear, due to a breakdown in love as a result of broken fellowship with God. "There is no fear in love; but perfect love casteth our fear; because fear hath torment. He that feareth is not made perfect in love" (1 John 4:18, KJV).

According to the above text, "Fear is thus caused by disturbances of love" (Pfister, 1948, p. 46). Adam and his wife were in a perfect environment (Eden) and dwelt in the presence of God. They had the peace of God, the provisions of God, and the power of God. Yet they did not obey God from the heart and the outcome was living in fear and a failure to fulfill the will of God. I really don't believe they were conscious of their new attitude of fear and the failure that was present and influencing their decisions. I also don't believe average Christians who confess faith in Jesus Christ are conscious that their lives are controlled by the attitude of fear and failure; they simply go through life without fulfilling their God-given purpose and never experiencing their full potential in God. I believe this because I use to be that kind of Christian and I know many who still are.

Since the first Adam's act of disobedience to God, mankind has been the slave of sin. As mentioned in the introduction, fear is a natural and normal emotion that all humans have. As a matter of fact, rational fear is a healthy emotion because it alerts us to danger, both in people and things that could cause injury, pain, or loss of life. Likewise, failing is a natural and normal experience that all people may encounter at some point in time in life. But to have irrational fear that results in illogical actions that lead to failure in doing the will of God, that is abnormal. Scripture says, "God has not given us a spirit of fear" (2 Tim. 1:7, KJV).

The apostle Paul declares, "I can do all things through Christ which strengtheneth me" (Phil. 4:13 KJV). Scripture also says, "If God be for us, who can be against us?" (Rom. 8:31, KJV). Now if God has not given His followers a spirit of fear, and if Christians can do all things through Christ who strengthens them and if God is for them; from whence comes this paralyzing doubt and potential-destroying, purpose-distorting fear? I say again, it comes as the result of sin, and Satan uses it as part of his schemes to produce very bad consequences and negative outcomes in the lives of mankind.

As I have already mentioned, some Christians still struggle with fear. I personally interviewed thirty adult men and women from ten mainstream denominations to gain further data about the specific types of fear that negatively affect them in their fulfillment of the will of God for their lives. I asked each person specific questions. I then recorded, evaluated, and interpreted the outcome of each question using a Fear

Assessment Tool (FAT) to determine fear categories. The data collected from the thirty individuals that participated in the sample group helped me to determine which of the five dominant psychological and irrational fears negatively affect Christians and hinder them in fulfilling the will of God for their lives.

In this section, I have entitled these irrational fears as dying fig leaves because the first Adam and his wife attempted to cover their nakedness with fig leaves because of fear. They acted in fear and attempted to cover themselves with fig leaves once their nakedness was revealed to them. Their problem then is the same problem that mankind has today. The condition of soul nakedness as result of sin cannot be cured nor covered by self-righteousness, nor human strength. Human effort will never cover or overcome sin or its outcome. Mankind's best attempt at righteousness apart from God's grace will always result in failure.

> "Thus saith the LORD; Cursed be the man that trusteth
> in man, and maketh flesh his arm, and whose heart
> departeth from the LORD" (Jeremiah 17:5, KJV).

In my research I discovered five dominant, irrational fears that keep some Christians from fulfilling the will of God for their lives. Dr. Karl Albrecht, author of the book *Social intelligence: The New Science of Success* states, "That there are only five basic fears (extinction, mutilation, loss of autonomy, separation, and ego-death), and that all other fears are just variations on these five themes." Dr. Albrecht defines fear as "anxiety associated with anticipating an imagined event or experience" (Albrecht, 2012, p. 19). Dr. Theo Tsaousides' version of these five fears are: "Fear of dying, fear of getting sick or injured, fear of losing control, fear of being alone and fear of hating yourself" (Tsaousides, 2015, p. 19). My version of these fears described by Dr. Karl Albrecht and Dr. Theo Tsaousides is listed below:

The Five Dying Fig Leaves of Fear

1) The fear of death
2) The fear of loneliness
3) The fear of loss
4) The fear of pain
5) The fear of rejection

These fears are internal and deeply rooted in the minds and emotions of people. They have been made a reality and reinforced by Satan through life experiences. I believe that some people, including Christians, are repeating the actions of the first Adam and attempting to cover their soul nakedness with dying fig leaves because of these fears.

The good news is that by the stripes of Jesus Christ, the child of God has been healed (Isa. 53:5). The Lord provided healing through His shed blood. Christ shed His precious blood not for the healing of the physical body, but for mankind to be healed in the soul, the seat of the will and emotions, imagination, and intellect. If you are a Holy Bible reader, you see that Jesus Christ was healing people of various kinds of diseases and physical ailments while He physically lived on earth. He was healing people physically before His blood was shed. If by His "stripes we were healed" meant physical healing, He would have needed to shed His blood before healing anyone during His earthly ministry. The stripes Christ received in His body and the blood He shed was for the healing of the sin-sick soul of mankind, for "without shedding of blood is no remission" (Heb. 9:22–26, KJV). The Scriptures do not say that without the shedding of blood there is no healing but that without the shedding of blood is no *remission*.

I want to be clear so there is no misunderstanding. I believe in physical healing by the power of God through the anointing with oil and prayer of faith by the elders of the church as Scripture declares (James 5:14–15 KJV), but this is not the context of Isaiah 53:5 (KJV). I have heard some people use this scripture as a basis for faith in physical healing, but I believe this is erroneous. Christ's shed blood provides healing for the soul of mankind, and God is able to heal and does heal people of physical ailments and sickness, as we can see clearly throughout the Holy Bible.

I believe that the soul is the place of warfare for the Christian, where some are losing the battle against Satan and sin daily. And though the Lord Jesus has purchased our freedom through His sacrificial death on the cross and His supernatural resurrection, some don't know how to appropriate the victory He has won. Satan therefore stealthily keeps them bound in a life of fear so they fail to fulfill the will of God for their personal and corporate lives within the Lord's Church. I was such a person in the past, but now I am free, and I want to expose the dying fig leaf–like actions of fear so others can have hope in overcoming their fear.

1. The fear of death (*thanatophobia*), is one of the most universal fears and may be the basis for many phobias. For example, "Individuals who fear darkness, choking, suffocation, enclosed places, flying in an airplane, epidemics, having a heart attack, developing cancer or acquired immune deficiency syndrome (AIDS), indirectly fear death under the other feared circumstances" (Doctor and Kahn, 1989, p. 123).

The fear of death is the first of the five prominent fears some Christians have. In my interviews with thirty sample group participants from ten major denominations; twenty-two of the participants struggled with the fear of death in their failure to fulfill the will of God for their lives. This fear and the others discussed later are the source of human attempts to cover ourselves with the failing actions of self-righteousness and human strength.

Martin Luther, founder of the Lutheran denomination, argues "That without the fear of the Lord, people think their good fortune is a result of their own merit and virtue" (Largen, 2011, p. 29). The Scriptures say, "Forasmuch then as the children are partakers of flesh and blood, he also himself likewise took part of the same; that through death he might destroy him that had the power of death, that is, the devil; And deliver them who through fear of death were all their lifetime subject to bondage" (Heb. 2:14–15, KJV).

> The fear of dying is when one is "literally afraid they are going to die, and their actions are going to lead them to extinction" (Tsaousides, 2015, p. 19).

Death came about as a result of the first Adam's disobeying God. Death is both a reality and mystery to mankind, and according to my research and interviews with some Christians, many still have great anxiety about death. However, followers of Christ need not fear because the Lord Jesus Christ has delivered them from the "sting of death" (1 Cor. 15:55–57, KJV). Physical death for the child of God is a transition from life in the flesh on the earth into everlasting life in Heaven with the Lord. "For if we believe that Jesus died and rose again, even so them also which sleep in Jesus will God bring with him. For this we say unto you by the word of the Lord, that we which are alive and remain unto the coming of the Lord shall not prevent them which are asleep. For the Lord himself shall descend from heaven with a shout, with the voice of the archangel, and with the trump of God, and the dead in Christ shall rise first; Then we which are alive and remain shall be caught up together with them in the clouds, to meet the Lord in the air; and so shall we ever be with the Lord. Wherefore comfort one another with these words" (1 Thessalonians 4:14–18, KJV).

For the person who does not know Christ as Lord and Savior, death is a haunting reality and a terrifying mystery that causes them to go to extreme measures to protect themselves with costly security devices and futile attempts to prolong their lives with pharmaceuticals and other scientific means. Some even seek to purchase peace of mind through false beliefs and erroneous religious practices that offer a fleeting but false hope of the afterlife. Because of the mystery and fear of death, some even deny the existence of God as the intelligent designer of the universe and believe that when human beings die, they simply cease to exist.

"St. Thomas Aquinas (1224–74) expressed a similar objection to the ontological argument. He believed the existence of God was self-evident and could not be deduced from arguments about the nature or character of God. Because we are finite humans with finite capacities for understanding, Aquinas argued that we can only understand finite concepts. Claiming that God is the greatest being that we can imagine or that exists, denial does not clarify the nature of character of God" (Kenny, 2015, p. 13).

I, however, believe Sigmund Freud and others like the four horsemen of modern atheism (Christopher Hitchens, Daniel Dennett, Richard Dawkins, Sam Harris) and many other atheistic thinkers fail to understand the simple principle of faith. Faith to believe in God comes from God and must be sustained by God for mankind to be able to trust in God. "He that comes to God must first believe that He is and that He is a rewarder of them that diligently seek Him" (Heb. 11:6, KJV).

God is real, He does exist and has revealed Himself in the person of Jesus Christ (John 1:1–3, 14). The life of Christ Jesus on earth and His death, burial, and resurrection are not just biblical or theological facts but recorded historical facts. The only thing that cannot be proven with concrete evidence outside of the "'textus receptus' or received text" is His bodily resurrection (Preslar, 2014, p. 13). However, I've seen the tomb in which He was buried and it is empty. Hallelujah! That, plus the abiding presence of the Holy Ghost in me, is enough evidence for me.

The good news is that Jesus Christ has delivered His children from the bondage that the fear of death causes. Christians don't have to fear death because Jesus Christ conquered death in the flesh. He died the death of sinful man and gave eternal life to those who will simply by faith believe in Him.

> But not as the offence, so also is the free gift. For if through the offence of one many be dead, much more

the grace of God, and the gift by grace, which is by one man, Jesus Christ, hath abounded unto many. And not as it was by one that sinned, so is the gift; for the judgment was by one to condemnation, but the free gift is of many offences unto justification. For if by one man's offence death reigned by one; much more they which receive abundance of grace and of the gift of righteousness shall reign in life by one, Jesus Christ.) Therefore, as by the offence of one judgment came upon all men to condemnation; even so by the righteousness of one the free gift came upon all men unto justification of life. For as by one man's disobedience many were made sinners, so by the obedience of one shall many be made righteous (Rom. 5:15–19, KJV).

2. The fear of loneliness, or being lonely, is known as *monophobia.* "This fear seems to increase with age as an individual sees friends and loved ones dying and anticipates having few contemporaries around. The fear of loneliness is compounded by the fear of illness" (Doctor & Kahn, 1989, p. 257).

In my research with thirty sample group participants, fifteen of them struggled with the fear of loneliness, which hindered them from fulfilling the will of God for their lives. The fear of loneliness is second in the list of some Christians' most daunting and dying fig leaf fears. The fear of being alone can also be defined as being "afraid of being abandoned by others and want[ing] to avoid becoming irrelevant, undesirable, disrespected, devalued, or disconnected" (Tsaousides, 2015, p. 19).

God made human beings to have fellowship with Him in His presence and for them to have companionship with other humans. It is not just the lack of human companionship that produces loneliness or the fear of being alone; it is the lack of fellowship with God the Creator that produces this fear of loneliness. God said, "It is not good that man should be alone; I will make a help meet for him" (Gen. 2:18, KJV). This is known as companionship. The Bible reader can see in Scripture that "the Lord God formed man of the dust of the ground, and breathed into his nostrils the breath of life; and man became a living soul. And the Lord God planted a garden eastward in Eden; and there he put the man whom he had formed" (Gen. 2:7–8, KJV). This is known as fellowship. God created man, God breathed into man the breath of life, and man became a living soul (a conscious being with will, desire, emotions, imagination, intellect). God then put the man in the garden He created. God created mankind in His image and likeness to first have fellowship with Him in the place God put him, the Garden of Eden (the presence of God). Companionship came later when God created the woman to be with the man.

Scriptures say that "In thy presence is fullness of joy; at thy right hand there are pleasures for evermore" (Ps. 16:11, KJV). In this messianic Psalm, the psalmist was saying that God the Father would not allow the soul of His only begotten son—Jesus Christ—to remain in hell, but that He would restore His life after His sacrificial death for the sin of mankind (resurrection) and bring Him back to the place of full joy and pleasure in His presence. This fellowship with God in His Presence is what God has provided for all His disciples through the atoning blood of Jesus Christ. Those who have the Son have this life and can enjoy the presence of God; they can have the peace and joy of God continually in any state of life. The child of God never has to feel lonely because the presence of God is a constant abiding presence in their lives as long as they remain in fellowship with Him. "If ye love me, keep my commandments. And I will pray the Father, and he shall give you another Comforter, that he may abide with you forever" (John 14:15–16, KJV).

Jesus Christ promises His obedient followers that they will never be without comfort because the Holy Spirit (the Spirit of truth, the Comforter) will abide with them forever. Again, this means the child of God who is obedient to the Word of God will never be alone, but it is not so with those who are not followers of Christ. The unbeliever has no fellowship with God in His presence. For the confessing believer, but non-professing believer, their fellowship with God can be and has potentially been broken through willful disobedience to God's Word as was the case with the first Adam. When this fellowship with God is broken, the person then experiences the void of God's presence and feels loneliness. Although he or she may have companions, when their fellowship with God has been broken, they will still feel lonely. I personally witnessed Christians who were in broken fellowship with the Lord attempt to cover their fear of loneliness with the dying figs of religious activities, while others used unhealthy, unbalanced, unauthorized, and sometimes abusive relationships with people and things that could never bring them the true fulfillment that comes only from being in habitual and consistent fellowship with the Lord in His Presence.

3. The fear of loss, or the fear of losing control, is the third in the list of fears of some Christians that cause them to fail to fulfill the will of God for their lives. The fear of loss is seen when one has an "irrational fear that they will not have what they believe is necessary for their physical and emotional well-being or they will lose these things" (Meinecke, 2018).

This fear of loss also involves the fear of losing one's beliefs or values. Fleming and Lovat, who are professors of theology and religion, use "the metaphor of leaving home to articulate a frequent experience of theology students who are invited out of the comforts of their 'home' worldview to consider that of others and who are at once 'feverish but also porous' in so doing" (Fleming & Lovat, 2015, p. 210). They speak of the anxiety that many students experience in being introduced to new beliefs and ideologies that are different from those of their childhood and the students' fear of losing what is of great value in defining their foundational religious beliefs. It is likened to the stress and anxiety one feels when leaving the familiar and protective environment of home and moving to a new residence in a different city where all people are strangers.

In my interviews with the sample group of thirty Christians, ten of the participants struggled with the fear of loss in their failure to fulfill the will of God for their lives. Scripture says that "whosoever will save his life shall lose it; but whosoever shall lose his life for my sake and the gospel's, the same shall save it. For what shall it profit a man, if he shall gain the whole world, and lose his own soul?" (Mark 8:35–36, KJV).

The Lord Jesus Christ gave this message to His followers so they could then and now understand the fear of loss. I believe God knows that loss is a real fear in the lives of people. He understands that individuals will go to great lengths to secure and safeguard the things they value. He taught His disciples and He presently teaches Christians through His Word what they should really value and what should be of great importance. He tells His followers to "seek first the Kingdom of God and His righteousness all these things shall be added" (Matt. 6:33, KJV). The things that He says shall be added to the followers of Christ who prioritize the will and ways of God are the things that the world (unbelievers) value. Unbelievers seek to protect and secure their possessions, such as investments, finances, homes, cars, clothing, food, companions, etc. because they fear they will lose them. They don't understand that because of the fear of loss, not only will they eventually lose all of their earthly possessions, but they will also lose the eternal life that Christ provided for them. Jesus says that those who attempt to save their worldly possessions in their own strength and ability will eventually lose them. For it is a fact, "that we came into the world with nothing, and it is certain that we will leave the world with nothing." (Gen. 3:19, Ecclesiastes 12:7, KJV)

The person who understands the eternal value of honoring God, doing the things that are pleasing to God, and promoting the gospel of Jesus Christ shall gain eternal life. They will also possess as a by-product of their obedience all the things that unbelievers are striving to gain and keep secure. The world fears loss and seeks to cover this fear by gaining and storing up more and more of what people think will bring them security and peace. The Christian must understand that everything they have comes from God. The earth is the Lord's and everything in it. "Behold, the heaven and the heaven of heavens is the Lord's thy God, the earth also, with all that therein is" (Deut. 10:14, KJV).

Christians must use wisdom and take precautions, such as securing valued possessions, locking doors and windows, and having alarms, insurance, savings, investments, etc. This is practical because we live in a sinful world, but most importantly, the child of God must trust God to keep that which He has given them the stewardship over as it relates to material possessions. Christians shouldn't value material resources in the same way non-Christians do. If the Lord does not keep and protect it, mankind certainly cannot, and we know that eventually all things in this world shall pass away. "Except the LORD build the house, they labour in vain that build it; except the LORD keep the city, the watchman waketh but in vain" (Ps. 127:1, KJV).

4. The fear of pain is the fourth in the list of fears that lead some Christians to failure in fulfilling the will of God. "Algophobia, odynesphobia, and odynophobia. Pain is a sensation that hurts enough to make one uncomfortable; it may be mild distress or severe discomfort, acute or chronic" (Doctor & Kahn, 1989, p. 297). Mankind has suffered and feared pain since the fall. "Although a wide variety of drugs are now available to ease pain, pain is still a fearful subject, and the prospect of having pain makes people anxious" (Doctor & Kahn, 1989 p. 297). I have not met anyone who enjoys or invites pain of any type, physical, psychological, or emotional. Pain is something that most people seek to avoid at almost any cost. I have learned over the years that I have high tolerance for physical pain, but even so, I still seek to avoid it. "When a person is injured, they begin to associate the injury with the activity that caused it, and they will avoid that activity—and other activities. In the short term,

avoidance may promote healing, but over time, fear of pain may actually initiate chronic pain, leading to disability and depression" (Volders, Boddez, De Peuter, Meulders, & Vlaeyen, 2015, p. 33).

In my interviews with thirty sample group participants, twenty-nine of the participants struggled with the fear of pain in their failure to fulfill the will of God for their lives. The fear of pain affects so many people to such an extent that their lives are controlled by avoidance. Some avoid going to the physician for a medical check-up because they fear the pain that may be required to cure their sickness. People who have been wounded or hurt emotionally fear the pain of loving or trusting again, so they avoid developing new and perhaps meaningful relationships. I know people who are professionally and self-medicated through prescription and/or illegal drugs because they fear the psychological pain of their present reality due to past decisions or damaging actions of others they trusted. The psalmist declares "If I had wings like a dove, I would fly away" (Ps. 55:12–14, KJV). Why? Because of the emotional and psychological pain that had been caused by the betrayal of one who was a friend and companion.

Some of the greatest pain that people experience is emotional and psychological due to the experiences they've had to endure in past or present relationships where there was or is an absentee parent, abortion, abuse, abandonment, adultery, divorce, poverty, or unexpected loss. I discovered during my interviews with some Christians that many admitted to engaging in avoidance due to some type of psychological and/or emotional pain.

The fear of pain can also be caused by strangers with whom we have no friendship or relationship by their actions, such as rape, robbery, senseless violence, injustice, oppression, murder, etc. The North Carolina State Bureau of Investigations reported in 2008 that one in eight American women had been the victims of attempted or completed rape in their lifetimes.

In other cases, pain is not caused by any person it's the pain of life. One example is the sudden unexpected death from a sickness or accident that was no one's fault. Such traumatic events and many more not mentioned can create emotional, physical, and psychological pain in the lives of people.

Jennifer Beste, author of *God and the Victim* challenges people to consider "the belief then that our ability (whether by freedom and/or grace) to respond to God's grace is not entirely vulnerable to earthly contingencies is firmly embedded in the Christian tradition. Does this longstanding, widespread conviction, however, remain credible in light of recent social scientific research on the insidious effects of severe, interpersonal injury to traumatized persons' identities and freedom? Should we not consider more carefully the possibility that we can harm one another to such an extent that someone's capacity to respond to God's grace can be severely diminished, if not altogether destroyed?" (Beste, 2007, p. 9).

I believe that after people have traumatic experiences, Satan seeks to capitalize on these experiences by creating irrational fears and unhealthy behaviors that keep them bound in cycles of addiction, aggression, and avoidance. As I mentioned earlier, there are Christians and non-Christians alike who are attempting to cover these pains of their souls in their own strength with dying fig leaves of false pretense and hypocrisy. There are people living in silent frustration and others whose lives are spiraling out of control because of the fear of pain. Despite these facts, the good news is that Jesus Christ is the healer of the soul and the Holy Spirit is the comforter. Scripture declares, "Come unto me, all ye that labour and are heavy laden, and I will give you rest. Take my yoke upon you, and learn of me; for I am meek and lowly in heart; and ye shall find rest unto your souls. For my yoke is easy, and my burden is light" (Matt. 11:28–30, KJV).

The Lord wants His followers to bring all of the pain of their past and present unto Him. When this happens, He gives His peace. When Christians commit to Jesus Christ and begin learning His Word and His ways, they will enjoy more and more of His comfort, joy, and peace in their lives. Children of God can and will learn to love and trust again. They can then establish wonderful and meaningful relationships, and in the areas where once hurt, they will be able to bring healing to others. Christians must decide to become victors instead of victims. This is possible for the child of God because the same Holy Spirit that was upon of Jesus Christ when He walked the earth is the same Holy Spirit that is now abiding within. Jesus declared, "The Spirit of the Lord is upon me, because he hath anointed me to preach the gospel to the poor; he hath sent me to heal the brokenhearted, to preach deliverance to the captives, and recovering of sight to the blind, to set at liberty them that are bruised, to preach the acceptable year of the Lord" (Luke 4:18–19, KJV).

The Lord Jesus declared that the Spirit of the Lord was upon Him not only to preach the gospel to the poor but also to heal those whose hearts have been broken through emotional and psychological pain and to proclaim freedom and liberty to those bruised and in emotional and spiritual bondage. So, not only has Christ provided healing and deliverance from the fear of pain for His children, but He has also given the same Spirit whereby freedom and liberty can be received and brought to others. "If ye love me, keep my commandments. And I will pray the Father, and he shall give you another Comforter, that he may abide with you forever; Even the Spirit of truth; whom the world cannot receive, because it seeth him not, neither knoweth him; but ye know him; for he dwelleth with you, and shall be in you. I will not leave you comfortless; I will come to you" (John 14:15–18, KJV).

5. The fear of rejection is the fifth and final fear that will be discussed in this list of fears among some Christians. "Fear of rejection is part of most social phobias. It is a fear of being socially excluded or criticized, which would produce considerable emotional pain and self-degradation" (Doctor & Kahn, 1989, p. 344).

In my interviews with thirty sample group participants, all thirty of the participants struggled with the fear of rejection in their failure to fulfill the will of God for their lives. "The fear of rejection is a powerful fear that often has a far-reaching impact on our lives. Most people experience some nerves when placing themselves in situations that could lead to rejection, but for some people, the fear becomes crippling. An untreated fear of rejection tends to worsen over time, gradually taking over virtually every part of a sufferer's life" (Fritscher, 2019).

I have experienced and witnessed the emotional pain of rejection and the many destructive attitudes and behaviors it creates, such as low self-esteem, abuse, addictive actions, avoidance, uncontrollable anger, jealousy, violence, and (what may be a surprise to some) tolerance. Some people tolerate physical, verbal, mental, and sexual abuse in destructive, toxic, and unhealthy relationships because their fear of rejection is greater than the pain inflicted by their abuser(s). The abused persons so desire to be accepted and not experience the pain of rejection that they are willing to tolerate negative and destructive acceptance over rejection.

I want to see if you can relate to the following scenarios as reported by two of the sample group participants of interviewed Christians. For the sake of keeping the interviewees names anonymous, they will be referred to as "John Doe and Susie Que."

John Doe reported that he saw a woman and he was attracted to her physical presence. He desired to approach her and introduce himself, but he felt nausea. The palms of his hands became sweaty, his feet felt like they were glued to the floor, and he couldn't move. He wanted to speak, but there was a lump in his throat. His mouth became dry and his voice vanished; therefore, he did not speak. What caused the physical symptoms that John Doe experienced? It was the fear of rejection. It wasn't that he did not want to approach the woman to whom he was attracted. He would have loved to have gotten to know her better and possibly began a stimulating conversation, but he feared being rejected. More dominant than the excitement of his attraction and potential happiness of meeting the woman of his dreams was the fear that she would not reciprocate his feelings and thus leave him with the daunting pain of being rejected.

Susie Que reported that she went to great lengths of personal sacrifice, anxiety, stress, and financial expense to plan a wonderful evening—a dinner at her residence to finally meet the parent(s) of the man she loves and believes will one day be her husband. She wanted the atmosphere, food, decor, entertainment, and all that was involved with the evening to be perfect. She became so stressed and anxious of the outcome that she was uncharacteristically abrasive and insensitive to her boyfriend and only thought of what she wanted at the time. Why did she feel so much anxiety? Why was her tolerance for error so low, and why was it that if everything didn't go according to how she had envisioned and expected, she would be so disappointed and potentially depressed? Why was she so consumed with pleasing people whom she'd never met? All of these feelings of anxiety and abnormal actions were the result of her wanting to be accepted. She feared that if things were not perfect, that she may be rejected by the parents of the one she loves.

At the time of the writing of this book, there is a popular weekly television show entitled *Catfish*. It's a show about two guys who travel all around the United States helping people find and meet face-to-face with the people they have established emotional relationships with online or in cyberspace via electronic devices. The people in these relationships have never met in person, but in all cases, they have been communicating and exchanging information about their lives, such as photos, occupations, hobbies, finances, fears, goals, dreams, and other intimate details. In some cases, the communication or relationships have been going on for years. In many cases, the two guys who arrange a face-to-face meeting between the individuals in these cyberspace relationships discover that some of these persons are not who they say they are. They are often lying and pretending to be someone they are not.

Why do so many people in these instances pretend to be who they really are not? Why do they steal the identity of someone else and present information that is not true to another person? Why do they seek to cover up and hide their true identity through false pretense and lies? It's not because all of them are bad or evil people who set out to hurt the ones they have deceived. It's not because they wanted to see if they could exploit another person for their own benefit and take what someone else has worked so hard to gain. In many cases, they are just ordinary people, young and old, male and female, from all walks of life and from various cultures and ethnicities. They are people who simply desire to be loved and accepted. The problem is that they fear being rejected, so they pretend to be someone they really are not. They hide and cover themselves in the darkness of hypocrisy to attempt to gain the acceptance of another. Again, the root cause of these actions and many more like them is the fear of rejection.

Rejection is one of the most dreaded pains that mankind experiences. People go to great lengths to avoid this pain. It's the pain of rejection that mankind desperately fears. I believe that Adam and his wife hid among the trees of the garden when they heard the voice of the Lord walking in the garden because they knew they had engaged in an action that would foster the Lord's disapproval. They feared being rejected by their Creator. God created mankind to experience His love and acceptance, but sin caused a breach in this loving and accepting relationship between mankind and their Creator. When sin rules in the life of mankind, there is a separation, and the enemy (Satan), the serpent of old, convinces them that God is no longer pleased with them; they are no longer accepted by God and they feel the pain of rejection.

The good news, however, is that Jesus Christ has paid the price for mankind's failure due to the sin of disobedience. He has once and for all bridged the gap that once existed between man and God because of sin. The first Adam and his wife did indeed feel rejection; they were cursed by God because of their disobedience to Him and they were driven from His presence. "Unto the woman he said, 'I will greatly multiply thy sorrow and thy conception; in sorrow thou shalt bring forth children; and thy desire shall be to thy husband, and he shall rule over thee.' And unto Adam he said, 'Because thou hast hearkened unto the voice of thy wife, and hast eaten of the tree, of which I commanded thee, saying, Thou shalt not eat of it; cursed is the ground for thy sake; in sorrow shalt thou eat of it all the days of thy life; Thorns also and thistles shall it bring forth to thee; and thou shalt eat the herb of the field; In the sweat of thy face shalt thou eat bread, till thou return unto the ground; for out of it wast thou taken; for dust thou art, and unto dust shalt thou return.' And Adam called his wife's name Eve; because she was the mother of all living. Unto Adam also and to his wife did the Lord God make coats of skins, and clothed them. And the Lord God said, 'Behold, the man is become as one of us, to know good and evil; and now, lest he put forth his hand, and take also of the tree of life, and eat, and live forever; Therefore the Lord God sent him forth from the garden of Eden, to till the ground from whence he was taken. So he drove out the man; and he placed at the east of the garden of Eden Cherubims, and a flaming sword which turned every way, to keep the way of the tree of life" (Gen. 3:16–24, KJV).

I want the reader to see a few truths in these passages of Scripture. God made coats of skins for them and covered their physical nakedness (Gen. 3:21). This is a picture and type of the atonement of mankind's sin by God Himself. In order for God to get the skin to cover Adam and his wife, something had to die. The animal from which the skin came to cover them had to be killed, its blood had to be shed and work had to be put into making the skins to cover them. Jesus Christ, the Lamb of God who took away the sin of the world, shed His blood and produced an atoning cover for the sin of mankind through His flesh. The Scriptures say, "Without the shedding of blood is no remission" (Heb. 9:22, KJV).

Adam and his wife didn't ask, beg, or plead with God to forgive them, nor did they do anything to earn or deserve what God did to cover their nakedness. God covered them because as the eternal Creator—Elohim (Gen. 2:4–25) and sovereign Lord (Gen. 15:2, 8)—God can do as He wills, when He wills, with what or whom He wills, where He wills, and how He wills because He and He alone is God. I believe that God also covered them because one His many characteristics is love.

He covered them because of His love for them. "He that loveth not knoweth not God; for God is love" (1 John 4:8, KJV).

> "The LORD hath appeared of old unto me, saying, 'Yea, I have loved thee with an everlasting love; therefore with lovingkindness have I drawn thee'" (Jeremiah 31:3, KJV).

The second truth in these passages of Scripture (Gen. 3) is that God never said to Adam and his wife, I am displeased with you, I no longer love you, I no longer accept you, I disapprove of you, and I reject you. God simply asked them a couple of questions: Where are you and have you eaten from the tree I commanded you not to eat from? *He* never rejected them. He dealt with them according to their actions as would any loving and responsible parent with their child or children. They were given consequences because of their disobedience; they were never rejected by God; they were disciplined by Him. I believe the feeling of rejection came as a result of sin, and Satan capitalized on it then, as he does now with so many people. The only reason given in Scripture as to why God drove Adam and his wife from the Garden of Eden was so they could not also eat from the tree of life (Gen. 3:21–24).

God could not allow them to do this because they could live in a rebellious and sinful state forever and never die. I also believe they were driven from the Garden of God because God is Holy, and nothing unholy, unclean, or unrighteous can abide in His presence. The point to emphasize here is that God didn't reject them; He disciplined them and followed through with what He said would happen when He first created them.

Later passages in scripture further establish that rejection did not come from God but as a result of sin and Satan's destructive work. The offspring of Adam and Eve were two sons, Cain and Abel (Gen. 4:1–7). Cain was a farmer and Abel was a shepherd. They both brought the Lord an offering from their work. God admired, esteemed, and looked with favor and respect upon Abel's offering from the flock, but He did not admire, esteem, or look with favor and respect at Cain's offering. Cain was displeased, angry, and emotionally upset because he didn't get the same response from God as his brother Abel. God saw Cain's dark disposition and I want you to notice what He (God) said to Cain, "But unto Cain and to his offering he had not respect. And Cain was very wroth, and his countenance fell. And the LORD said unto Cain, 'Why art thou wroth? And why is thy countenance fallen? If thou doest well, shalt thou not be accepted?'" (Gen. 4:5–7, KJV). God didn't reject Cain personally. He didn't accept what Cain brought Him. God then gave Cain instructions on what to do so his offering would be accepted. But like many people who feel rejected and experience emotional pain, Cain allowed the desire of sin to overtake him, and he further rebelled against God by allowing his anger, which was being fueled by the feeling of rejection to move him to kill his brother Abel. "And Cain talked with Abel his brother; and it came to pass, when they were in the field, that Cain rose up against Abel his brother, and slew him" (Gen. 4:8, KJV).

Through the disobedience of one man, sin entered the world of mankind. It is also true that by the "obedience of one [Jesus Christ] shall many be made righteous" (Rom. 5:19, KJV). Because of Christ's obedience to God the Father through the shedding of His blood for the remission of mankind's sin, their consciences can be purged from dead works to serve the living God (see Hebrews 9:14). This should help Christians understand that, in Christ they can live without a guilty and shameful conscience, and serve the Lord with great joy and peace knowing that they are fully pleasing and acceptable to Him through Jesus Christ. No longer does the child of God have to fear rejection.

Chapter Five

THE FIVE FAILING TREES
OF SATAN'S WORLDLY SYSTEM

And he said, Who told you that you were naked?

In Genesis, the Word of God says that after Adam and his wife disobeyed God, their eyes were opened and they knew they were naked. Not only did they cover themselves with fig leaves, they hid among the trees of the garden. "And they heard the voice of the Lord God walking in the garden in the cool of the day; and Adam and his wife hid themselves from the presence of the Lord God amongst the trees of the garden" (Gen. 3:8 KJV).

In this section, I discuss another outcome of fear as a result of sin, which is *hiding*. When mankind's mindset or thinking is dominated by the attitude of fear, the result is hiding (covering up, pretending, avoidance, pride and self-reliance). Not only do people seek to cover the nakedness of their souls with dying fig leaves, they also go into hiding. This hiding involves the false hope and evaporating illusions that Satan offers in his worldly system. The first Adam and his wife hid among the trees of the garden, and I believe that people with the Adamic nature are still hiding and pretending today. They are not hiding among physical trees in the forest or wilderness, no these trees are different; they have been grown and developed in the soil of the systems of the world in which mankind abides.

In this section, I discuss five trees that mankind is still hiding among as a result of fear. These are not physical trees like the ones the first Adam and his wife hid among, but they are emotional, mental, and psychological, but yet are just as real as physical trees. Satan has planted and grown these trees in the system of this world, and he offers them as hiding places for people who are blinded by his deception and ensnared by his schemes.

> "But if our gospel be hid, it is hid to them that are lost;
> In whom the god of this world hath blinded the minds
> of them which believe not, lest the light of the glorious
> gospel of Christ, who is the image of God, should shine
> unto them" (1 Cor. 4:3–4, KJV).

> "Wherein in time past ye walked according to the course
> of this world, according to the prince of the power of
> the air, the spirit that now worketh in the children
> of disobedience; Among whom also we all had our
> conversation in times past in the lusts of our flesh,
> fulfilling the desires of the flesh and of the mind; and
> were by nature the children of wrath, even as others"
> (Eph. 2:2–3, KJV).

Satan is the god or ruler of the systems of the world in which all mankind has to operate within. He is the prince of the power of the air. This is why our Lord Jesus Christ prayed for His followers. "I have given them thy word; and the world hath hated them, because they are not of the world, even as I am not of the world. I pray not that thou shouldest take them out of the world, but that thou shouldest keep them from the evil" (John 17:14–15, KJV).

The Lord has prayed for followers and He is at the right hand of the Father making intercession for His disciples. "Who is he that condemneth? It is Christ that died, yea rather, that is risen again, who is even at the right hand of God, who also maketh intercession for us" (Rom. 8:34, KJV). I want to emphasize that the true followers of Christ are going to be okay. There may have been some lost battles and casualties, but Christians can be confident in the fact that "in Christ we are more than conquerors." (Rom. 8:37, KJV). So until then, I encourage Christians not to hide among the trees of the world but stand firm and fight the good fight of faith in Jesus Christ.

The first tree of the world that Satan offers to hide among is the:

Tree of Performance

Satan wants people to think that their identity, self-worth, and even their acceptance by God comes from performance. He tricks many into believing they can be saved or come into right standing with God based upon performance. He wants people to believe that God loves and accepts them based upon their performance. Nothing could be further from the truth. God's love and acceptance of us is not based upon performance. Nor does value or self-worth come from performance. Some people may have experienced environments or people who accepted, loved, and valued them based upon performance, but this not how God loves. God loves and accepts sinful man based upon the atoning blood of Jesus Christ—the righteous one. This is why once a person is in Christ, he or she is forever loved and accepted by God—no more performing, no more pretending, and no need for stubborn pride or the ability of self. The truth is that God hates performance because it makes the sacrifice of Christ worthless.

The value of something is determined by what someone is willing to pay for it. God established mankind's value Himself because Jesus Christ was willing to lay down His life to purchase mankind from the slave market of sin. God the Father gave His best (His Son, Jesus Christ). He paid the debt of sin through His atoning blood and granted freedom through the gift of salvation. It was freely given, and mankind can freely accept it and be made righteous through the blood of Jesus Christ. Love, mercy, grace, forgiveness, and acceptance are gifts from God to man. They cannot be earned or purchased. Salvation is by grace through faith. It is the gift of God and no one can boast or accept any credit for what God alone has done. Stop performing and stop hiding among the tree of performance.

> "For by grace are ye saved through faith; and that not of yourselves; it is the gift of God; Not of works, lest any man should boast" (Ephesians 2:8–9, KJV).

The second tree of the world that Satan offers to hide among is the:

Tree of Pleasure

Satan wants people to indulge in all the pleasures of this world. He uses worldly pleasures to entice, entrap, and enslave people. There is an old motto in the world: If it feels good do it. This is the mindset of people who are bound in sin and enslaved by the god of this world. Many people suffering from emotional pain and spiritual darkness attempt to use pleasure as a remedy for the pain of their souls. This is futile and usually leads down a path of wrong decision-making that produces some type of addiction, debt, deception, divorce, or other destructive behavior. I want the reader to understand that God is not against having fun and enjoying the pleasures of this life that He (God) has provided mankind. There are many things in the world that are enjoyable and produce great pleasure with no negative strings attached. God has given Christians all spiritual blessings in heavenly places in Christ Jesus, and He wants them to enjoy them all. "Blessed be the God and Father of our Lord Jesus Christ, who hath blessed us with all spiritual blessings in heavenly places in Christ" (Eph. 1:3, KJV).

However, Christians have to be careful as the apostle John writes "Love not the world, neither the things that are in the world. If any man love the world, the love of the Father is not in him. For all that is in the world, the lust of the flesh, and the lust of the eyes, and the pride of life, is not of the Father, but is of the world" (1 John 2:15–16, KJV). There are some things in the world that appear to be blessings of the Lord, but in reality, they are entrapments of Satan. The Scriptures say, "The blessing of the Lord, it maketh rich, and he addeth no sorrow with it" (Prov. 10:22, KJV).

The pleasures God gives do not have any sorry or regret attached to them. If the pleasure involves fleshly indulgence, such as coveting, pride, lust, excessive debt, lying, cheating, hurting, dishonoring, breaking of covenants, stealing, killing, etc., they are not of God. These are the pleasures of the world, and they are satanic traps. Christians should avoid them at all costs. I want you to know that if someone you know or even you yourself are entrapped in these worldly pleasures, please seek help and get out of them. The Word of God says that the end result of living according the carnal (fleshly) mind will produce death. "For to be carnally minded is death; but to be spiritually minded is life and peace" (Rom. 8:6, KJV).

The Word of God also says that there is pleasure in sin, and Christians should learn from the example of one of the great leaders in the Holy Bible, Moses. Moses was unwilling to enjoy the pleasures of Egypt (a type of the world), but chose to suffer with the chosen people of God (Heb. 11:25).

Followers of Christ must do the same; instead of yielding to the pleasures of sin that come from Satan, they must stand for and enjoy righteousness, peace, and joy in the Holy Ghost. The child of God can be confident in knowing that he or she is under the rule or authority of God and they need not hide among the worldly tree of pleasure.

> "For the kingdom of God is not meat and drink; but righteousness, and peace, and joy in the Holy Ghost. For he that in these things serveth Christ is acceptable to God, and approved of men" (Rom. 14:17–18, KJV).

The third tree of the world that Satan offers to hide among is the:

Tree of Popularity

In this informational, technological, media-driven culture, there are many people who want to be popular, such as actors, athletes, entertainers, politicians, and yes even preachers. It seems that everyone wants to be popular. It doesn't matter if they are right or wrong, liked or disliked, honored or dishonored, as long as it produces popularity or fame. The use of technology and the ability to photograph or record live and instantly post or share through the vehicle of social media only makes the idea of popularity even more of an epidemic. Some people will do almost anything to become popular. I believe that this is a great factor for why people young and old, Christian and non-Christian, from various cultures and ethnicities struggle with peer pressure. The societally induced pressure to be liked and accepted and to fit into what and who is popular is driving people into all types of ungodly and dysfunctional actions. People are willing to go to great lengths and pay great costs to be popular.

The tree of popularity in this world is another one of Satan's schemes to enslave and destroy the souls of people. Christians should not yield to the temptation of this satanic vice. I believe that if the Lord wants a person to be known, seen, or heard, then He will lift and exalt them. Christians should not seek to be popular because this is as futile or as hopeless as one trying to catch the wind in their hands. Popularity cannot and will not bring fulfillment for soul pain.

The Word of God says, "Except the Lord build the house, they labour in vain that build it; except the Lord keep the city, the watchman waketh but in vain" (Ps. 127:1, KJV).

This verse of Scripture says that if anything is done in the ability of self and for self, it is vain or for nothing. If God does not promote or make popular, it is not necessary. Christians must learn to be content with such as they have. I intentionally used the word "content," which involves, "being at peace, satisfied, and having joy within oneself" (Merriam-Webster Dictionary). I believe Christians should never stop pursuing all that God has for them and that they should seek to experience everything that God has created them to do. I am not advocating settling for less than God's best as followers of Christ. I am stressing, however, that they should not strive according to the world's definition and standard of success.

If God has made or makes the Christian popular in whatever career field they work and with what talents they possess, great. I believe God puts people where He needs and wants them for His purpose and plan. I believe that if a Christian has a platform or position of popularity, they should use it for the honor and glory of God. The point here is that the most important thing for Christians is not to seek to be known by men but seek to know and be known by God. This was the Apostle Paul's desire; he wanted to get a firm grip on the One (Jesus Christ) who had gripped His heart and changed His life.

For my determined purpose is that I may know Him [that I may progressively become more deeply and intimately acquainted with Him], perceiving and recognizing and understanding the wonders of His Person more strongly and more clearly, and that I may in that same way come to know the power outflowing from His resurrection [which it exerts over believers], and that I may so share His sufferings as to be continually transformed [in spirit into His likeness even] to His death, [in the hope] That if possible I may attain to the [spiritual and moral] resurrection [that lifts me] out from among the dead [even while in the body.] Not that I have now attained [this ideal], or have already been made perfect, but I press on to lay hold of (grasp) and make my own, that for which Christ Jesus (the Messiah) has laid hold of me and made me His own (Phil. 3:10–12, AMP).

The apostle Paul demonstrated that he didn't need or want the world's popularity; he wanted more of a passion to know and be conformed into the image of Jesus Christ. That should also be the desire of all followers of Christ—not to be popular in this world, but to know and be known by Christ. Don't seek popularity, don't put much time and energy into trying to be popular in this world because this world and all that's in it is passing away and will one day be completely gone. I strongly admonish Christians not to seek to be popular, and if they are to please stop. I challenge the popularity-driven Christian to come out from among this tree of the world because it cannot and will not satisfy the thirst of the soul.

> "And they that use this world, as not abusing it; for the fashion of this world passeth away" (1Corinthians 7:31, KJV).

The fourth tree of the world that Satan offers to hide among is the:

Tree of Possessions

In this modern society and culture, many people equate value with material possessions. They derive personal value from their material possessions. I believe this is why there are so many people attempting to hide among the tree of possessions. They are seeking to cover the pain of their souls and their nakedness with material possessions. Satan uses this tree to deceive many and give a sense of security, but the security is false.

In the Word of God, we can learn from the wisest, richest, and most influential person on earth in his time—Solomon, the king of Israel. He used his riches, position, and power to explore all the pleasures of the world. There was nothing that his heart desired that was withheld from him. He amassed great possessions, far beyond what any man can even begin to imagine. Yet at the end of his life, having seen it all and done it all, he declares it is all vanity:

> I sought in mine heart to give myself unto wine, yet acquainting mine heart with wisdom; and to lay hold on folly, till I might see what was that good for the sons

of men, which they should do under the heaven all the
days of their life. I made me great works; I builded me
houses; I planted me vineyards; I made me gardens
and orchards, and I planted trees in them of all kind of
fruits: I made me pools of water, to water therewith the
wood that bringeth forth trees: I got me servants and
maidens, and had servants born in my house; also I had
great possessions of great and small cattle above all that
were in Jerusalem before me: I gathered me also silver
and gold, and the peculiar treasure of kings and of the
provinces: I gat me men singers and women singers, and
the delights of the sons of men, as musical instruments,
and that of all sorts (Eccl. 2:3–8, KJV).

Solomon concludes that all of one's labor and all that one possesses
will one day be left to another and he will have no control over what
they do with all of life's labor.

Yea, I hated all my labour which I had taken under the
sun; because I should leave it unto the man that shall
be after me. And who knoweth whether he shall be a
wise man or a fool? Yet shall he have rule over all my
labour wherein I have laboured, and wherein I have
shewed myself wise under the sun. This is also vanity
(Ecclesiastes 2:18–19, KJV).

Solomon concludes that it is an empty endeavor to seek to amass
possessions here on earth because no one, no matter how wealthy, powerful, or prominent, can take any material possessions with them once
they die. Mankind brought nothing into the world, and it is certain that
we can carry nothing out. I again emphasize that God is not against
material possessions, nor is having a lot of material possessions wrong or
evil. However, some seek to gain their sense of identity and value from

their possessions. So, in reality, they don't have material possessions; they are possessed by materials. Jesus told His followers not to store up treasures here on earth that will rust and decay and that thieves will steal, but rather store up treasures in heaven that will not rust and decay and that thieves cannot steal. The terminology "store up" refers to amassing for future security. Material possessions can only give false security; real security can only come from God.

> "Lay not up for yourselves treasures upon earth, where moth and rust doth corrupt, and where thieves break through and steal; But lay up for yourselves treasures in heaven, where neither moth nor rust doth corrupt, and where thieves do not break through nor steal; For where your treasure is, there will your heart be also" (Matt. 6:19–21, KJV).

Material possessions cannot give life and they don't add value to the possessor of them. The owner adds value to the possessions. God has given people the things of this earth to freely enjoy for the benefit of mankind, not for mankind to be bound to or enslaved by. Yet there are many who are depressed, indebted, devoid of values, divorced from their families, stressed, sick, and enslaved; some have even sacrificed their own lives in order to continue hiding among the tree of possessions. I believe that this too is another one of Satan's diabolical schemes to blind people and keep them from knowing their true purpose, power, and potential. All the possessions in the world cannot purchase security for our souls. This can only be found in Jesus Christ, the One who gave His life so mankind can be free from the bondage of sin. Mankind, Christians and non-Christians alike, should stop trying to cover the nakedness of the soul and stop trying to quench the thirst and satisfy the hunger of the soul with the possessions of the world.

"For what is a man profited, if he shall gain the whole
world, and lose his own soul? Or what shall a man give
in exchange for his soul" (Matthew 16:26, KJV)?

The fifth tree of the world that Satan offers to hide among is the:

Tree of Position

People seek positions that are prominent and important in every
culture. If society says the position is of value, the masses strive to be
in that place. If the culture says the position is to be desired, the world
places a certain monetary value on the position. I believe that many
people value money and for some, money is a god, so they covet positions with high monetary payoffs. They think their position gives them
their identity and their value. This is why in some conversations with
people with whom acquaintance is sought, the question is: What do you
do for a living? In other words: What is your position in society? Based
upon the predetermined value of the position in the societal system of
the world, there is a tendency to attach this value to the person. This
is how people often relate to one another. They unconsciously judge or
determine value or worth based upon the position a person holds.

I believe the need of mankind to cover the nakedness of their souls
because of fear drives many to attempt to hide behind their position in
society. The more valuable and honorable the position, the more value
the person in the position derives. But again, this is a false value and
satanic deception. Christians must realize that what the world values,
is not what God values. God does not value, honor, and esteem people
based upon their positions in the world's system. The child of God
should not develop an attitude of pride or arrogance because of position.
They should also not develop an attitude of inferiority or low self-esteem
because their position is not honored or highly esteemed in the world.
Christians should learn to be content with and love the position they
have, while always pressing to be the people God created and gifted

them to be. I also advise to be content, but never settle. If one strives to be in a certain position for the wrong reason, he/she will never be fulfilled in that position. This is why so many people change their life's work, careers, and positions. There is a false belief and false hope that the right position will give them what they desire in life. The position may give the social status and money, but the position and money cannot give correct status or more value with God.

Christians should work as unto the Lord and seek to reflect the image of Christ in whatever position they hold in society. The position does not make them; they make the position. Again, their value and identity has already been determined by God.

Jesus Christ said to His disciples that the people in the highest positions in the world treat those who are under them as not having much value or importance. Jesus said to them that this must not be your attitude. As a matter of fact, if you are in the highest position according to the standards of the world, do the opposite of those who hold these positions. He said become the servant of those who are in the lower positions. He said to them, "I am your Lord, Master, Chief; I hold the highest position; yet I am among you as One who serves" (Luke 22:27 KJV).What a difference between how God sees positions, attitudes, and actions and how the world views them.

> "And he said unto them, 'The kings of the Gentiles exercise lordship over them; and they that exercise authority upon them are called benefactors. But ye shall not be so; but he that is greatest among you, let him be as the younger; and he that is chief, as he that doth serve. For whether is greater, he that sitteth at meat, or he that serveth? Is not he that sitteth at meat? But I am among you as he that serveth'" (Luke 22:25–27, KJV).

Jesus Christ tells His followers that the highest calling and the most prominent and valuable position in His Kingdom is to be a servant. In the worldly culture, the servant is regarded as the lowest and least in value. Christians must make sure that their values are Christ-centered and not culture-centered. This is why Satan wants Christians to strive for positions in his system. Doing so puts them in direct conflict with God's way. So, no matter what your position is in this society, seek to be the greatest by having a servant's attitude and servant actions in your life's work. In so doing, you will come out of hiding among the tree of position in this world.

Chapter Six

OVERCOMING FEAR AND FAILURE

And he said, Who told you that you were naked?

In Genesis 3:9–11, the Bible records a very interesting and important dialogue between Adam and God. The Lord God called to Adam and asked him a question: "Where are you?" Adam did not answer the Lord by telling Him his location; he told Him his state of mind and perception of himself. Adam said, "I heard thy voice in the garden, and I was afraid, because I was naked; and I hid myself" (Gen. 3:10, KJV).

God is omniscient (all-knowing) and omnipresent (everywhere). I believe God knew Adam's location because He sees and knows all. He is almighty God, the eternal Creator [Elohiym—H430] (Strong, 1984). God was not seeking Adam because He did not know where he was. I believe God wanted Adam to realize where he was. Why? Adam didn't know where he was and he had lost his way. It was Adam who had broken fellowship with God through his rebellion against the revealed will of God. It was Adam who was no longer fulfilling his purpose. It was Adam who did not understand the gravity of his disobedience. It was Adam who was hiding from God. It was Adam who had run away from God, instead of running to God. It was Adam who was behaving perversely and living in false pretense. It was Adam who had succumbed to Satan's diabolical plan, and Adam was being controlled by fear as a result of sin.

As aforementioned, I believe these actions were caused by irrational fear as a result of sin. I believe fear continues to create similar actions in the lives of people presently. Again, this is why I believe many Christians struggle to fulfill the will of God for their lives.

God was fully aware of what Adam had done. He was not taken by surprise because of the action of disobedience by Adam then, nor is God surprised by the actions of mankind now. It was God who created Adam. It was God who created the woman as a helper for him. It was God who created fellowship with mankind in the Garden of Eden before their disobedience, and it was God who re-established fellowship with Adam and his wife after their disobedience. God came seeking Adam after the fall, and it was God who started speaking to Adam after the fall. Adam didn't go seeking the presence of God after his fall. Adam didn't ask for forgiveness for his disobedience to God. There was nothing in Adam that sought God in his sinful state, nor is there anything in sinful man that seeks after God now. It was, is and always will be God and God alone. It is God who continues to seek mankind and restore fellowship with him, even while in sin. However, it is what God does and says to Adam in Genesis 3:11 that's important in understanding how to overcome fear.

> "And he said, 'Who told thee that thou wast naked?
> Hast thou eaten of the tree, whereof I commanded thee
> that thou shouldest not eat?'" (Genesis 3:11, KJV).

I want you to pay close attention to what is about to be discussed. Scripture says, "And they were both naked, the man and his wife, and were not ashamed" (Gen. 2:25, KJV). This is the last verse of this chapter and helps us understand how God created the woman as a helper for the man He created. This chapter also shows Adam declaring how a man and woman should establish and grow in the covenant relationship of marriage. It finally shows the state of mind of the man and the woman before their disobedience (Gen. 3). Scripture says, "The man and his wife were both naked and not ashamed" (Gen. 2:25 KJV). The Hebrew word used for naked in this passage of Scripture is the word *arowm* [H6174], which means "to be nude, either partially or totally" (Strong, 1984, pg. 91).

Again, the Scriptures say that before disobeying the command of God and sinning against God, humans were nude (bare skin) either partially or totally and felt no shame, no embarrassment, no guilt, no condemnation, no negativity, no anxiety, and no fear.

The next time the word "naked" is used in Scripture is in Genesis 3:7. Adam and his wife have partaken of the fruit of the tree that God commanded them not to eat of, and "the eyes of both them were opened and they knew they were naked" (Gen. 3:7, KJV). The Hebrew word used for naked in this passage of Scripture is the word *eyrom* [H5903 and H6191], which means "nudity" and carries the connotation to be cunning; usually in a bad sense; to deal subtly or crafty; it carries the negative connotation of guilt and shame (Strong, 1984, pg. 88, 92).

Scripture says that for the first time since being created, since having been given dominion, governance, and authority on earth; since operating in their God-giving purpose; and since enjoying unbroken fellowship with God in His presence, mankind became aware of how to be subtle and crafty, experienced and had feelings of shame, guilt, condemnation and irrational fear. Mankind experienced nakedness.

They covered themselves with fig leaves and hid among the trees of the garden. Adam said to God, "I was afraid, because I was naked; and I hid myself" (Gen. 3:10, KJV).

I believe what Adam said to God is the same thing that many Christians are saying to Him from their souls. The reason I am running away from You instead of running to You, is that my fellowship with You is broken. The reason I'm attempting to live independently from You is because I'm no longer depending on You. It is why I am pretending to be someone that I am not and why I am failing to fulfill Your will for my life. My emotions and psychological state are abnormal and perverse because I am naked. I feel like my life has no purpose. I feel like I have no potential and no power. I feel like a failure, a victim of life's circumstances. My thoughts are unclear and confused; my emotions are in a whirlwind. The pressures of life are overwhelming, and to make matters worse, I now question if You are who You say you are. I'm having real difficulty trusting that You love me and care for me. When I fail You, I feel rejected by You.

Again, I believe this was the thinking of Adam after sinning against God, and I believe this is the present state of many Christians attempting to live outside of fellowship with God. It is the state of mind that Satan desires Christians to remain in although they confess to know God.

The great news, however, is what God says to Adam "And he said, 'Who told thee that thou wast naked?'" (Gen. 3:11, KJV). God asked Adam a question, and it is the same question the Lord asked me over thirty years ago after I accepted Him as Lord and Savior, and I became a Christian. The Lord asked me, even as He asked Adam, "Who told you that you were naked?"

The Lord challenged me to examine the source of every thought, emotion, and action that caused me to fear and believe that I was a failure. Now, under the power of the Holy Ghost, I am asking you the reader and Christians throughout the body of Christ who are failing to fulfill the will of God in their lives to do the same.

I believe this is the time for fearful and failing Christians to hear what God, their God, who created them in His image and likeness, is saying to them. It is God who sent His Word to heal (Ps. 107:20). It is Jesus Christ, the Savior of the world who has provided healing for the souls of mankind from the destruction of sin by His atoning death for sin (Isa. 53:5).

I believe God is now seeking and speaking to His followers. God is asking a very powerful question: "Who told you that you were naked"?

Who told you that you have to live in fear, guilt, shame, or condemnation?
Who told you that your life has no purpose?
Who told you that you were a mistake?
Who told you that your life has no meaning?
Who told you that you don't have potential?
Who told you that you are powerless?
Who told you that you are a victim?
Who told you that you are unlovable?
Who told you that you are unattractive?
Who told you that you are rejected?
Who told you that you are confused?
Who told you that you are a failure?
Who told you that God is not trustworthy?
Who told you that God doesn't love you?
Who told you that God is not with you?
Who told you that you could not be forgiven?
Who told you that you are all alone?
Who told you that dreams don't come true?
Who told you that you would not succeed?
Who told you to stop trying?
Who told you that peace, love, and joy are not for you?
Who told you to live in defeat?
Who told you live in misery?
Who told you to accept "no"?
Who told you to live in mediocrity?
Who told you that you couldn't be great?
Who told you to quit or give up?
Who told you to stop loving?
Who told you to stop trusting?
Who told you all men are alike?
Who told you all women are alike?
Who told you that you are going to be hurt?
Who told you to be defensive to avoid being hurt?

Who told you to stop giving?

Who told you to stop living?

Who told you to stop believing?

Who told you to stop achieving?

Who told you that you were not good enough?

Who told you that you don't have value?

Who told you that you are good for nothing?

Who told you that you cannot change?

Who told you that God made a mistake?

Who told you that you born that way?

Who told you that you should give up?

Who told you that you would die?

Who told you that you should stop trying?

I could go on and on, but the reality is you are not what you have come to believe, feel, think, or experience if what you believe, feel, think, or experience is contrary to what God says. The Lord is asking now what He asked Adam in the beginning: Who told you that?

God didn't tell Adam and his wife they were naked. They did not get that information from God. It came from the voice of fear that originated with their sin. Adam felt that way because his fellowship with God had been broken by sin. And all people, born with the Adamic nature, think, feel, and behave the same as he did when fellowship with God was broken because of sin. My earnest hope and prayer is that you, the reader, and Christians everywhere can hear the voice of the Holy Spirit saying, "I did not tell you that you were naked."

Christians must understand that fear has a voice and failure is a choice. When fellowship with God is broken and the voice of fear says, "God is displeased and He is only interested in judging you," it is a lie from Satan. God is only displeased with His children when they allow fear to rob them of the faith God has given to trust Him. "But without faith, it is impossible to please God" (Heb. 11:6, KJV).

The feeling of rejection causes mankind to choose a path of failure by attempting to cover up and hide through self-righteousness, hypocrisy, or trying to avoid God all together by denying His existence or rebelling against His Word. I believe all people can come out of hiding when they allow the Lord to cover them in His righteousness. In Christ, all people can overcome and walk in total victory. Now is the time to break the curse and abound in blessings. Today is the day to hear the voice of God, come out of the grave of spiritual death, mental defeat and emotional despair. It is time to live.

> "Marvel not at this; for the hour is coming, in the which all that are in the graves shall hear his voice, and shall come forth; they that have done good, unto the resurrection of life; and they that have done evil, unto the resurrection of damnation" (John 5:28–29, KJV).

I understand that the above passage speaks of the resurrection of life for the righteous and the resurrection of damnation for the unrighteous after the millennial reign of Christ spoken of by the Apostle John in Revelation 20:7–15. But after Martha, the sister of Lazarus said, "I know that he will rise again in the resurrection at the last day" (John 11:24, KJV), Jesus said to her, "I am the resurrection and the life. He who believes in Me, though he may die, he shall live. And whoever lives and believes in Me shall never die. Do you believe this?" (John 11:25–26, KJV).

I am saying to my fellow Christians today what the Lord said to Martha concerning her dead brother Lazarus: If you believe in the Lord, you can and will live right now. The child of God can come out of whatever type of grave fear has caused them to live in—if they will simply allow Christ Jesus to restore their broken fellowship with Him through His blood and start hearing His voice. He is the Resurrection and the Life, and He will speak life into the dying soul and spirit.

I don't know who laid Lazarus in his physical grave, but I do know that fear has laid many people in emotional, mental, and psychological graves. I also know that when God's presence came in the person of Jesus Christ to the tomb of Lazarus and he heard the voice of the Lord, he came forth. Lazarus came out of a physical grave and overcame physical death when He heard the voice of Christ. How much more can Jesus Christ, who is the same yesterday, today, and forever, call His followers forth into new life? Just as Lazarus heard and came forth unto new life in Christ, I believe Christians can overcome fear by hearing the voice of the true and living God. The Holy Spirit is now saying "Come forth." Christians should not allow fear to bind and blind them any longer. Today is the day to hear the voice of the Lord and overcome fear. Today is the day to decide to fulfill the will of God in every area of life, because the Lord is asking, "Who told you that?"

Chapter Seven

FIVE PRACTICAL KEYS TO OVERCOMING FEAR AND FAILURE

And he said, Who told you that you were naked?

I). *Read* the Word of God daily.

The patriarch Job said, "Neither have I gone back from the commandment of his lips; I have esteemed the words of his mouth more than my necessary food" (Job 23:12 KJV).

What conviction and what a declaration from one of the heroes of the faith. The Bible reader can now better understand how Job could go through the disaster of all disasters involving disease, death, division, despair, and destruction in his personal life and family, but yet remain faithful to God. He questioned God, but he did not fall away from God. He did not allow the thought of failure to abide in his mind. Why? Because of the Word of God that was in him. Job held the Word of God in high esteem in his life, even more of a necessity than food. I assume Job ate food every day, as most people do. The physical body needs nutrition and energy that good, healthy foods provide to develop, empower, and grow, so it can remain strong and healthy. A healthy body can overcome sickness and disease, and the immune system can fight and defeat different types of diseases that try to enter and use the internal organs as agents of destruction. Food causes growth through the building of muscle mass and strengthening of the skeletal structure. Food is a vital necessity for all living creatures.

Job says, however, that the Word of God is more important. This is why Christians must consume it daily. How is this done? It cannot be eaten physically like a sandwich, salad, or steak, but the Word of God can be consumed and ingested by reading, studying, and meditating upon it. The child of God must take the sixty-six books of the Holy Bible and consume them daily, esteeming it as essential to spiritual, psychological, mental, and emotional well-being. The Holy Bible must be ingested in the soul and spirit just as good nutritious food is for the physical body. In the pages of the Holy Bible, the Christian will discover the principles, precepts, and promises of God. The Word of God, read daily, will help to overcome fear and strengthen the faith and resolve of believers so they can fulfill God's will for their lives. Christians can gain so much wisdom, understanding, and knowledge from the Word of God. It will help them become successful in every area of life when read, studied, and applied.

Reading the Word of God is foundational in learning to hear and recognize the voice of God versus the voice of fear. As previously stated, fear has a voice and fear speaks the language of doubt and unbelief. Fear will continue to speak unless it is silenced by the truth of the Scriptures. As Christians begin the good habit of reading the Scriptures daily, their understanding of God's word will become clearer. Their understanding of Scripture will become broader and deeper, as will their ability to hear and discern the voice of God. I want Christians to know that God's voice will never contradict His written Word. If the child of God has the Holy Bible, he/she has God's word. God can and will speak from Scripture. Any voice that contradicts the Holy Bible is not the voice of God and it should not be followed. Reading the Word of God daily will sharpen the spiritual senses and enhance the desire for truth so much that the Christian will be able to recognize the error, heresy, false doctrine, false teachers and false prophets of the world. The Word of God will stabilize and strengthen their spirit, soul, and body so that the voice of fear that attempts to lead down a path of failure can be silenced. When the Word of God is believed, received, and practiced by the Christian, it will equip, empower, and punish fear for daring to speak. It will put failure to shame for attempting to stop such a Word-conscious, set-apart, sin-defeating saint of the most high God. In order to habitually live in this type of overcoming victory of fear, read the Word of God daily!

II). *Remain* in the presence of God.

The psalmist declares, "Thou wilt shew me the path of life; in thy presence is fullness of joy; at thy right hand there are pleasures for evermore" (Ps. 16:11, KJV).

Joy comes from being in the presence of the Lord, and the Scriptures also say, "The joy of the Lord is our strength" (Neh. 8:10, KJV).

This means the more time spent in God's presence, the more joy received. The more joy received, the more spiritual, mental, and emotional strength. The stronger the Christian becomes in these areas, the more empowered and enabled they are to overcome fear and failure and fulfill the will of God for their lives. Here are a few biblical practices for habitually and consistently remaining in the presence of God.

The first practice for remaining in the presence of God is to *walk* with God. You may ask: How does one walk with God? It is simple, but not easy. The Scriptures say, "And Enoch walked with God; and he was not; for God took him" (Gen. 5:24, KJV).

I believe that Enoch accompanied, spent time with, obeyed, and enjoyed unbroken fellowship with God. He did this so much that he was more equipped for heaven than for earth, so God took him to His heavenly home without experiencing death. Christians can also walk with God, accompany Him, and enjoy unbroken fellowship with Him when they make a practice of reading and studying God's Word so that they obey, love, and live according to God's Word consistently and habitually. The Word of God will transform the person who obeys it into to the image of Jesus Christ. It will also transform the mind, so the obedient doer can have the mind of Christ. It protects believers from the evil in the present world and prepares them for the pleasures in the world to come. Abiding in the Word of God causes the child of God to remain in the presence of God. According to Scripture; "In the beginning was the Word, and the Word was with God and the Word was God" John 1:1, KJV).

When Christians walk through the Word of God by reading, studying, and obeying it, while motivated by a heart of love for God, they are walking with God. The Word (Jesus Christ) is with God (the Father), and the Holy Spirit who abides in the follower of Christ will "guide them into all truth" (John 16:3, KJV). As they walk in the Word of God, the Father and the Son come in and make their dwelling in the spirit of the obedient doer of the Word. "Jesus answered and said unto him, 'If a man love me, he will keep my words; and my Father will love him, and we will come unto him, and make our abode with him'" (John 14:23, KJV).

The abiding presence of God in the person who loves God and keeps (walks) in His word is the Holy Spirit (the Spirit of truth, Advocate, Comforter, Counselor, Helper, Intercessor, Strengthener, and Standby). As Christians love, read, and obey the Word of God, they remain in the presence of God, and His presence remains in them in the third person of the Godhead—the Holy Spirit. They also get to enjoy all the wonderful attributes of His character, which include truth, advocacy, comfort, counsel, help, intercession, strength, support, and guidance.

The second biblical practice for remaining in the presence of God is to *work* for God. The people who give of their talents, time, and treasures in service to God have the promise that His presence will be with them. Christians remain in God's presence, and God's presence is with them when they work to fulfill His will on earth. It is God's desire that His will be established on earth as it is in heaven. "Thy kingdom come. Thy will be done in earth, as it is in heaven" (Matt. 6:10, KJV). The Lord also tells His followers, "All power is given unto me in heaven and in earth.

Go ye therefore, and teach all nations, baptizing them in the name of the Father, and of the Son, and of the Holy Ghost. Teaching them to observe all things whatsoever I have commanded you; and, lo, I am with you always, even unto the end of the world. Amen" (Matt. 28:18–20, KJV).

When Christians are willing to go forth and work for God in the service of proclaiming His Word and making disciples of all nations, God promises to be with them always, even unto the end of the world. God's presence, power, and provisions are wherever His will is being accomplished by His willing servants. The Scriptures describe "How God anointed Jesus of Nazareth with the Holy Ghost and with power; who went about doing good, and healing all that were oppressed of the devil; for God was with him" (Acts 10:38, KJV).

When Jesus was on earth, He worked to fulfill the will of the Father who had sent Him, and the Father's presence was with Him. If Christians want to remain in the presence of God and have His presence with them, they must decide and dedicate their talents, time, and treasure to the work of God. Jesus declares "I must work the works of him that sent me, while it is day; the night cometh, when no man can work" (John 9:4, KJV).

The Lord tells His followers in this passage of Scripture that there will come a time when no one will be able work for Him. I strongly admonish Christians to get busy working for God by serving in their local church. Use the talents and gifts God has given you to serve the Lord and others so they can see good works and glorify the Father in Heaven. "Let your light so shine before men, that they may see your good works, and glorify your Father which is in heaven" (Matt. 5:16, KJV).

Don't allow anyone or anything stop you from working for the Lord. Work while you can, when you can, and wherever you can. Work in whatever capacity He allows, and make sure you work unto Him, not to be seen or rewarded by people. God is looking for laborers and He will use you in His service if you are willing to work for Him.

The third practice for remaining in the presence of God is to *worship* God. The Scriptures say, "But the hour cometh, and now is, when the true worshippers shall worship the Father in spirit and in truth; for the Father seeketh such to worship him" (John 4:23, KJV).

Worship is the third biblical practice for remaining in the presence of God. The Father seeks for those who worship Him in spirit and truth. I believe that when God finds true worshippers, He establishes His dwelling in the place where praise to Him is being offered according to Psalm 22:3. He remains in them and the worshippers remain in Him. This creates a continual cycle of love, adoration, honor, praise, thanksgiving, value, and worth that is shipped to God by the worshippers through acts of obedience, love, service, and sacrifice. In return, God's presence gives the worshippers joy, purpose, pleasure, peace, provisions, protection, and total fulfillment, which creates more love, adoration, honor, praise, thanksgiving, value, and worth in the worshipper, which they in turn send to God, and the cycle goes on and on and on. This delightful cycle between worshippers and God continues until God decides to take these worshippers from the realm of earth to Heaven. Through a life of worshipping God, the Christian becomes more equipped for Heaven than earth, as did Enoch (Gen. 5:24).

The worshippers of God must have a heavenly body in order to live in Heaven. God therefore prepares a celestial (heavenly) body, because the terrestrial (earthly) body is for the earth. When the time comes for worshippers to make the transition or trip to Heaven, God allows them to fall asleep (die) or to be "caught up" according to Scripture (1 Thess. 4:14–17). When this happens, the earthly body can go back to earth from whence it came, and the true worshippers can put on the heavenly body that was made for living in Heaven. I believe that God does this because there is more room in His heavenly home for His worshippers than there is in their earthly home. In the terrestrial house, God is limited as to what He can do in and through His worshippers. But in His heavenly dwelling, He is unlimited as to what He can do in and through His worshippers. The Lord takes His true worshippers home to dwell with Him so they can experience all the wonderful and inexpressible pleasures of reigning and ruling with Jesus Christ in the Father's Presence forever and ever.

III). *Renew* your mind through meditation on the Word of God.

If Christians are going to be successful in overcoming fear, not only must they read the Word of God daily and remain habitually in the presence of God, but they must also transform their thinking. This is known practically as making an attitude shift. For some people, it will involve minor attitude adjustments, but for others it will require a major attitude overhaul. The apostle Paul speaks about the importance of making this attitude shift. "I beseech you therefore, brethren, by the mercies of God, that ye present your bodies a living sacrifice, holy, acceptable unto God, which is your reasonable service. And be not conformed to this world; but be ye transformed by the renewing of your mind, that ye may prove what is that good, and acceptable, and perfect, will of God" (Rom. 12:1–3, KJV).

I believe that if the child of God wants to understand the will of God to fulfill it as one who worships and works for God, it will require a total commitment and dedication to God. Once this decision of total commitment to God is made, the mindset, thinking, or attitude will have to go through a change, metamorphosis, or transformation. The believer's mindset, thinking, beliefs, and perception of life must align with the Word of God. God's Word and God's way have to become the top priority. This adjustment and transformation has to be chosen by each individual believer and follower of Christ. This is why the apostle Paul says, "I beg of you fellow, followers of Christ to present your bodies" (Rom. 12:1, KJV). He understood, as Christians today must understand, that our attitude about life is a choice. If there is going to be a change, it will require a choice—an active, deliberate, dedicated commitment to obey the Word of God. The Word of God is the key to changing the old, darkened, and destructive mind created by all the experiences of a life of sin into a mind that is full of light and life through a personal relationship with Jesus Christ. This renewal of the mind or change in thinking takes place as Christians meditate upon the Word of God.

Meditation upon God's Word is a deliberate and decisive action of taking the truth (practices, precepts, principles, and promises) of the Scriptures and pondering, questioning for clarity, seeking to understand, studying, and injecting oneself into them for the purpose of memorizing and modeling. The Christian must think about the Word of God, until the Word of God becomes the foundation of all other thoughts, beliefs, and actions. Replace old ideologies, experiences, feelings, and practices with new, God-filled, faith-filled, joy-filled, peace-filled, love-filled, honor-filled, and service-filled ideals, feelings, and experiences as proclaimed and practiced in the Word of God.

In the beginning of creation, before man's disobedience to God that resulted in sin, mankind once possessed this type of God-filled attitude and outlook on the life. When fear entered the attitude of mankind, the God-filled attitude was lost. Through fellowship and knowledge of God obtained through faith in the atoning work Jesus Christ; mankind can once again attain God's attitude or what is known as "the mind of Christ" (1 Cor. 2:16, KJV).

It is not enough for the believer to say, "I have faith in God." Christians must read the Holy Bible and remain in the presence of God by walking with, working for, and worshipping God. They must also make a conscious choice to renew their minds by the Word God.

I liken the renewal process to a water purification system similar to the one I have at my residence. The water purification system separates the unwanted and unhealthy particles from the water, so my family and I can ingest only pure water without any contaminants. I believe that Christians must likewise choose to filter every thought, experience, feeling, perception, attitude, and action of their lives through the purification system of the Word of God, so only those things which are good, acceptable, and perfect will remain. When this happens habitually and consistently, the child of God will find that their minds are renewed and their ability to understand, articulate, communicate and carry out the will of God for their lives is enhanced. This new attitude will help to overcome the old attitudes of fear anytime it rears its ugly, unwanted head. I encourage Christians to choose to be transformed by the renewing of their minds, and in doing so, overcome fear and start fulfilling the will of God for their lives. Allow this new, Christ-like attitude to begin with this truth and declaration, "I can do all things through Christ which strengtheneth me" (Phil. 4:13, KJV).

IV). *Risk* loss when godly rewards are possible.

I love the Bible story of the Prophet Elijah and the widow of Zarephath (1 Kings 17:9–16). The story involves a widow woman, whose name is not mentioned. She is a single parent on a fixed income that is just about completely spent because of a terrible economy. She has no family, no government aid, and no community agency assistance because the entire country is in a great economic depression. She's outside gathering a few sticks to kindle a fire to prepare the last meal for herself and her son. After this meal, they will probably die of starvation. I can imagine that she is afraid, angry, depressed, and in deep despair because of her plight in life. It's unknown as to whether or not she has prayed and asked God to intervene, but it appears that her situation is hopeless.

The story also involves a man, but not just any man—a man of God, a prophet of God to the nation of Israel by the name of Elijah. I must inform and remind you that the reason the entire nation was in such economic distress was because of what the prophet said, by the authority of God. He said it would not rain for a period of three years. The reader may wonder why? Elijah only did what God told him to do. The lack of rain was God's way of punishing the nation of Israel for their idolatrous practices, disobedience, and rebellion against Him. At that period of time, the nation of Israel was agrarian, which means their main source of income and livelihood came from what they grew and harvested from the land. No rain for three years created a deadly and dire condition known as famine.

This story also involves God, the God of Israel, who tells His prophet Elijah to leave where he is and go to the city of Zarephath because He (God) has commanded a widow there in the city to provide for his needs. I believe God has a sense of humor because He sent Elijah, his prophet, to a poor widow who was also a single parent with no income and no resources. God told Elijah that she was the one who was going to provide for him during a famine. If I were in Elijah's shoes, my rational mind would think that God was joking. I may even be tempted to ask, "Lord you have to be kidding, right?" But here again I strongly emphasize, this is why our human minds must be renewed, so we can do as Elijah did, trust God even when it seems laughable.

Another reason I love this story is because it involves fear versus faith, doubt versus trust, disobedience versus obedience, profit versus loss, and risk versus reward. Elijah, the prophet, had to trust God, and the widow had to trust him. She had to fight the fear of what she was seeing, feeling, and experiencing. She had to have faith and trust what the man of God said. We don't know if she was a worshipper of God or not, because the city of Zarephath was a pagan city, and its citizens were known to practice the worship of Baal. It is possible that the widow may not have been a worshipper of the God of Elijah at all. God may have sent Elijah to her house to save more than just her physical life and that of her son. He may have sent him there to save their souls from spiritual famine and death. Whatever the reason, she had to choose to have faith and trust what the man of God said.

She had to choose to take a risk and possibly lose what she had in order to gain the reward of a prophet and profit in a way that could change her life. I want the reader to understand that this story speaks of real people, in real life, with real decisions and real consequences. Just like the widow in this story, Christians must learn to overcome fear by being willing to risk losing what they have in order to be rewarded with that which can change their lives. When God speaks, the child of God must learn to trust and obey Him by faith.

Hans Urs von Balthasar says, "Faith, love, hope must always be a leap for the finite creature, because only in that way does it correspond to the worth of the infinite God. It must always mean taking a risk, because God is worth staking everything on, and the real gain lies, not in a 'reward' for the daring leap, but in the leap itself, which is a gift of God and thus a share in his infinitude" (von Balthasar, 1989, p. 145).

When God gives an instruction to follow, profit is always possible, even if what seems necessary is lost. Do not fear taking the risk to obey God. When a reward is possible through an act of obedience, be willing to take the risk. I'm not saying to take foolish, unplanned, uncalculated, misguided, or emotional risks. No, I'm referring to good, sound counsel that is full of wisdom based upon good facts and/or truth from the Word of God.

If you've been hurt emotionally, you will have to risk being hurt again in order to be healed and discover companionship. In order to grow financially and become profitable, you will have to risk investing, although what is invested has the potential of being lost. The investments or business may gain great profits, or all could be lost, but to do nothing is to be controlled by fear.

Christians must be willing to learn what they don't know, get what they don't have, go where they have not been, and become what they are not. Dare to be the person God created you to be. Decide to be better, not bitter or bound. Tap into the gifts and talents lying dormant within. Do as the late Dr. Myles Monroe said, "Don't let the grave rob you of your potential" (Dr. Myles Monroe). The child of God can overcome fear and defeat failure. Take good risks and enjoy godly rewards. Live out what the Word of God says, "If they obey and serve him, they shall spend their days in prosperity, and their years in pleasures" (Job 36:11, KJV).

I know and understand that you may be ridiculed and misunderstood, but you will be in good company. No one accomplishes anything great and noteworthy by playing it safe all the time. Dare to risk losing comfort and convenience in obedience and service to God in order to gain the reward of a life of prosperity and pleasure in God's presence. I challenge Christians to risk loss when a God-given reward is possible.

V). *Run* toward your giant.

The Holy Bible contains one of the most exhilarating and fascinating stories of the underdog being triumphant over what is seemingly a formidable foe. It is the story of David and Goliath (1 Sam. 17:1–51). David was a young teenage shepherd boy given the assignment of keeping watch over his father's sheep. It's a job that no one really wanted because the hours were long, conditions were deplorable, and the pay was terrible. To make matters worse, the job was very dangerous and potentially deadly. David was the youngest of eight brothers born to his father, and as the youngest, shepherding was his responsibility. His older brothers served in the army of Israel. To the average person, David was probably the most improbable person to solve the national crisis facing the nation of Israel during that time. However, there was something about David that made him different from his brothers and the rest of the men serving in the army of Israel. David was anointed. He had a special endowment of God's grace, power, and presence upon his life. That anointing equipped and empowered him to overcome life's challenges and negative circumstances.

Goliath, a Philistine from Gath, was a gigantic man who stood just shy of ten feet tall. He wore a bronze helmet on his head, his coat of scaled body armor weighed approximately 125 pounds, and he had a javelin across his shoulders, a spear as tall as a telephone pole with an iron spearhead that weighed approximately twenty pounds. He was a great warrior who had been fighting since he was a youth. His stature blocked the light of the sun, his voice reverberated, and when he walked, the ground shook beneath him. He and the army of the Philistines were standing facing the armies of Israel who were opposite them with a valley between the two armies.

The two nations prepared to go to war with each other, but instead of all the men fighting each other, Goliath proposed that just two men fight one another. Israel's best and bravest warrior was challenged to fight against him. If that man was able to defeat him, then the Philistines would admit defeat and serve the Israelites, but if Goliath won, then Israel had to admit defeat and serve the Philistines. That was Goliath's proposal for forty days, and no man in the entire army of Israel was willing to step forward and face the challenge because of fear.

I want to ask you as the reader: Have you ever faced a circumstance, situation, or problem so big, so daunting, so, seemingly impossible that the very thought or sight of it was emotionally, mentally, physically, and/or spiritually paralyzing? If your answer is "Yes," you may be able to empathize with the feelings of the entire army of Israelite warriors when they saw and heard the giant named Goliath in the story.

I spoke of a young shepherd boy named David at the beginning of this discourse. In the story, David was on his father's assignment, so he went to see how his brothers were doing and to bring food and supplies to the men in the army. David was simply being obedient to what his father told him to do. When he arrived, he heard and saw the giant defying the army of Israel. David decided to do something about it. The anointing of God upon his life was agitated, and he decided he was going to put a stop to Goliath's rhetoric. So, he announced to all the men present that he would fight the giant.

I believe that after David made the decision to fight him, he envisioned defeating him, so he declared to him how God was going to deliver him into his hands. But what I find more interesting than all of these things in this fascinating story is this: "And it came to pass, when the Philistine arose, and came and drew nigh to meet David, that David hasted, and ran toward the army to meet the Philistine" (1 Sam. 17:48, KJV).

I believe that at this time, David didn't know if he was going to win or lose, or live or die, but when the giant he faced moved toward him, David ran toward the giant. David didn't allow Goliath's stature, voice, age, armor, experience, or words to paralyze him in fear. He moved. He shifted from where he was and ran toward this giant. David did not allow the fear of failing to keep him inactive, uninvolved, disengaged, living beneath his potential, or hiding in false hope, self-pity, or guilt. I say the child of God or believer in Christ shouldn't either. David tapped into the anointing that was upon his life. He silenced fear, shackled failure, and shifted into the freedom that the power and presence of God provided.

I believe that like David, Christians can and will do the same as they realize that they are on their heavenly Father's assignment. The anointed one, Jesus Christ, abides in them and His ability is upon their lives. The child of God is not facing or fighting life's battles alone. God is fighting for His followers, and no one or nothing can be against them. I make a bold declaration of faith that you the reader and Christians abroad are now ready to run toward and defeat your giant of fear and failure. The voice of Goliath taunted the men of Israel for forty days, and there may be Christians who have been taunted forty days, weeks, months, or years. However long it has been, enough is enough. Now is the time to move forward and once and for all to overcome fear and failure, because the Lord is with you. He is fighting for you and He is now asking you the question: ***Who told you that?***

WORKS CITED

Albrecht, K. (2012, March 22). *"The (only) Five Fears We all Share"*. Psychology Today. Retrieved from psychologytoday.com/blog/brainsnacks/202203/the-only-5-fears-we-all-share

Beste, J. E. (2007). *God and the Victim*. Oxford, NY: Oxford University Press.

Braha, H. (2004). *Freeze, flight, fight, fright, faint: Adaptationist perspectives on the acute stress response spectrum*. CNS Spectrums, 9(9), 679–685.

Collier, A. (2003). *On Christian Belief—A Defense of a Cognitive Conception of Religious Belief in a Christian Context*. London and New York: Routledge.

Conklin, E. G. (2011). *Thirteen Americans: Their Spiritual Autobiographies*. In L. Finkelstein (Ed.). New York.

Doctor, R. M., & Kahn, A. P. (1989). *The Encyclopedia of Phobias, Fears and Anxieties*. New York, NY: Facts On File, Inc.

Finkelstein, L. (2011). *Thirteen Americans—The Spiritual Autobiographies*.

Fleming, D., & Lovat, T. (2015, July). *Learning as Leaving Home: Fear, Empathy, and Hospitality in the Theology and Religion Classroom*. Teaching Theology & Religion, 18(3).

Fritsher, L. (2019). *Fear of Rejection Behaviors and Consequences.* Verywell Mind.

Gurnall, W. (2014). *The Christian in Complete Armour—Volume I.*

Imbach, J. (1984). *Living in Anxiety?* Chicago, Illnois: Franciscan Herald Press;.

Kenny, D. T. (2015). *God, Freud and Religion.* New York, NY: Routledge.

Largen, K. J. (2011). *The Role of Fear in Our Love of God: A Lutheran perspective.* Wiley Periodicals and Dialog, Inc.

Meinecke, L. (2018). *The Uncanny Fear of Loss, Part 1: Losing the Unthinkable .* Theory and Praxis—Wikimedia.

Pfister, O. (1913). *The Psychoanalytic Methods—3.* London: Kegan Paul, Trench, Trubner & Co. Ltd.

Pfister, O. (1948). *Christianity and Fear: A Study in History and in the Psychology and Hygiene of Religion.* London, Great Britain: Unwin Brothers Limited.

Preslar, T. W. (2002). *An Introduction to the Study of Bible Doctrine.* Mineral Springs, NC: Gospel Schools of The Bible.

Preslar, T. W. (2014). *An Introduction to the Study of New Testament Greek—Part One—The Introduction and Philology.* Mineral Springs: Gospel Schools of the Bible.

Simpson, A. B. (2011). *The Self Life and the Christ Life.* E-Books.

Strong, J. (1984). *The New Strong's Exhaustive Concordance of the Bible: With Main Concordance, Appendix to the Main Concordance, Key Verse Comparison Chart, Dictionary of the Hebrew Bible, Dictionary of the Greek Testament.* Nashville: Thomas Nelson Publishers.

Tetsola, J. (2001). *Prophets and Prophetic Leaders.* Bogota, NJ: End Time Wave Publications; .

Tsaousides, T. (2015). *Brainblocks: Overcoming the 7 Hidden Barriers to Success.* New York: PRENTICE HALL PRESS.

Volders, S., Boddez, Y., De Peuter, S., Meulders, A., & Vlaeyen, J. (2015). *The Journal of Pain.* Pergamon, 64.

Von Balthasar, H. U. (1989). *The Christian and Anxiety.* San Francisco: Ignatius Press.

Zodhiates, Spiros, (1984, 1991). *Hebrew-Greek Key Word Study Bible King James Version.* Chattanooga, TN: AMG Publishers

Zondervan. (1987). *The Amplified Bible, Expanded Edition.* Grand Rapids, Michigan: Zondervan Bible Publishers

CPSIA information can be obtained
at www.ICGtesting.com
Printed in the USA
FSHW020722170720